AS Drama and Theatre Studies: The Essential Introduction for Edexcel

South Sefton
6th Form College

AS Drama and Theat ... *e Essential Introduction* ... *Edexcel* comprehensive and a ... e to the new specification. The textbook covers all aspects of the ... epth, from exploring play texts to demonstrating skills in performance and theatre design. The detailed guidance and classroom-friendly features include:

- overviews of specification and assessment requirements;
- written and practical exercises;
- tips from a chief examiner;
- extension activities to stretch the more able student;
- worked examples to illustrate best practice;
- a glossary of useful words and terms.

Written by a chief examiner and a principal moderator, this authoritative book offers a wealth of informed and supportive exercises to ensure that students reach their maximum potential.

Alan Perks is a chief examiner. He regularly works with students and teachers across the key stages on individual projects and long-term drama strategies. He also teaches across the age ranges, including the A Level course, part-time in a school in Derbyshire.

Jacqueline Porteous is a principal moderator, with over twenty years of teaching experience in the discipline. She teaches the A Level course and leads a Performing Arts Faculty.

AS Drama and Theatre Studies: The Essential Introduction for Edexcel

South Sefton
6th Form College

ALAN PERKS AND JACQUELINE PORTEOUS

Routledge
Taylor & Francis Group

LONDON AND NEW YORK

First published 2009
by Routledge
2 Park Square, Milton Park, Abingdon, Oxon OX14 4RN

Simultaneously published in the USA and Canada
by Routledge
270 Madison Ave, New York, NY 10016

Routledge is an imprint of the Taylor & Francis Group, an informa business

Typeset in Charter by Keystroke, 28 High Street, Tettenhall
Printed and bound in Great Britain by MPG Books Ltd, Bodmin

British Library Cataloguing in Publication Data
A catalogue record for this book is available from the British Library

Library of Congress Cataloging-in-Publication Data
Perks, Alan, 1956–
    AS drama and theatre studies : the essential introduction for Edexcel /
    by Alan Perks and Jacqueline Porteous.
        p. cm.
    Includes index.
    1. Theater. 2. Theater—Production and direction. 3. Drama.
    I. Porteous, Jacqueline, 1961– II. Title.
    PN2037.P44 2009
    792.071—dc22   2008013906

ISBN10: 0–415–43658–3 (hbk)
ISBN10: 0–415–43659–1 (pbk)
ISBN 13: 978–0-415–43658–8 (hbk)
ISBN 13: 978–0-415–43659–5 (pbk)

Contents

Illustrations

Acknowledgements

The authors would like to thank the Drama Department and drama students at the Ecclesbourne School, Derbyshire, for all their creativity and hard work, with particular reference to the class of 2007 and the class of 2008. Thanks to Jake Waring for worked example suggestions and technical solutions!

Thanks also to Edexcel for supporting the book and to the many drama teachers who have shared their thoughts with us along the way.

Finally, a word of thanks for those who have quietly supported from a distance with a cup of coffee or glass of wine and to our respective four-legged friends for never forgetting when it was time for a walk.

The authors and publishers would also like to thank the following for their kind permission:

- BBC Bitesize for permission to reprint a short extract on *An Inspector Calls.*
- The *Guardian* and Michael Billington for permission to reprint short extracts from the *Guardian* website.
- Kneehigh Theatre Company, Emma Rice and Steve Tanner for permission to reprint an interview with Emma Rice and five photographs from the company's productions.
- Scott Graham, Steven Hoggett and Frantic Assembly for permission to reprint a photograph from *Pool (No Water).*
- Simon Higlett, Stagework and the Birmingham Repertory Theatre for permission to reprint the set design image from *The Crucible.*
- Jacqui Addams, Sarah Bailey, Claire Beecroft, Rebecca Blake, Yasmin Bruce, Sarah Butler, Joshua Calladine, Ton Cudworth, Freya Donaldson, Rebecca Douglas, Rachel East, Emily Guard, Georgina Hayes, Lee Hayward, Hannah Meredith Hemmings, Jake Henry, Charlotte Jackson, Anthony Januszewski, Kerry McCabe, Lauren Madeley, Emily Maskell, Katy O'Brien, Maya Rafferty, Rachel Salisbury, Gemma Smith, Monty Till, Alex Wall, Jake Waring, Martin Weston, and Paul Willers for their permission for images of their rehearsals and performances to be reprinted.

GETTING STARTED   PART I

1 Introduction

It is always good to know where we are coming from at the start of a course, and one of the first things we need to do is to establish very quickly what we understand 'drama' and 'theatre' to mean.

For our purposes, drama is mainly concerned with the process of exploring and is about using a range of techniques to access the given material, often in workshop activities, and theatre is about engaging an audience through a range of performance techniques and elements following a period of preparation and rehearsal.

The Edexcel GCE Drama and Theatre Studies Specification states that:

The AS year requires you to demonstrate knowledge and understanding of:

- A minimum of two published plays demonstrating understanding of how style, form, dramatic structure and characterisation can be interpreted and realised in performance, and how plays relate to their historical, social and cultural context – they must be varied in terms of period and genre.
- The work of at least one influential **director**, **designer**, theatre company or other practitioner who has made a significant contribution to theatre practice.

How do we go about it then?

The important thing to remember is that you have chosen Drama and Theatre Studies and you will have had a good reason for doing so. Look around you. All the other people in the room will have good reasons for being there too – perhaps the same as yours, perhaps not, but think about this:

You are all in this together.

Those people sitting around you are going to support you in getting the grade you want from this course, and you will be doing the same for them. Drama and Theatre Studies is about being part of a group, actively engaged

director
The person in control of all aspects of the production, primarily in relation to the actors but also responsible for the ideas to inspire the design considerations to support the overall vision. Most directors will work collaboratively but will exercise the right to have the final say.

designer
Responsible for creating the look and feel of the production. There are usually a number of contributors to design in the professional theatre, each responsible for a particular aspect of design, including set, lighting and costume.

in a range of activities. If you wanted a subject where you work much more on your own, then you should not have chosen this course.

It has to be said right from the start, and very clearly, that there was absolutely no point in choosing this subject if you are going to find it difficult to work with others. If you think that this is going to be the case, then you need to close this book, pick up your bag and quietly slip out of the room now.

Should you decide to stay – and we hope you do – then the good news is that this course is all about *you,* but it is not about you in isolation. Nobody ever did well in drama working in isolation. This course is about you in relation to others and nobody in the room around you can succeed without you all working together and getting to grips with the demands of the subject at this higher level of study.

Cast your mind back to your experience of drama to date. You will almost certainly have had drama at Key Stage 3 and, perhaps, even at primary school. You may belong to a youth theatre or amateur dramatics group or perhaps attend a provider such as Stagecoach on a regular basis, all of which feeds very well into your current decision to develop your interest, understanding and qualifications further at this level of study. Many people taking Drama and Theatre Studies will have followed an examination course at Key Stage 4. GCSE was great, and it was probably your best or equal best grade, encouraging you to want to take the subject now. You will have learned an awful lot that you can use on this A-Level course, but, and this is the important bit: you have to move on.

You cannot sit back on your GCSE laurels and expect the AS course to fall into your lap and the excellent grade to follow. It would be like an athlete saying I won a race once or a footballer saying I scored a goal last season. It is not enough to have done it. What you need to do now is to keep on doing it and finding new ways of extending and developing your knowledge of theatre and performance and your place within that in relation to this higher national standard. We hope you will be challenged by the course and that you will rise to the challenge, pushing your self harder in order to achieve more.

Some things about the course will be more straightforward than others, and some activities will engage you more effectively, but, at every stage, you need to be looking to focus on the task, be clear about what you need to do, and get on with it. We hope this textbook will help you in the structuring of your work.

2 Making good use of this textbook

There are a few basic facts about the course that you need to be clear about before you go any further. These will help you to access the course and to make good use of this textbook. In Unit 1, your teacher is also your assessor with responsibility for marking your contribution to the unit against the published criteria. Your teacher will be leading you into the unit with an understanding of what is required in order for you to be able to access the marks. Every task set, therefore, will be set for a purpose and with the assessment criteria in mind. There is no time for a sloppy response to anything; you must remain focused at all times and keep an eye on deadlines your teacher may set for you.

You must meet your deadlines – so that your teacher can meet deadlines that are set by the Exam Board and are final.

In Unit 1, the deadline for the final submission of work is set each year by the Examination Boards, and, except under exceptional circumstances, there is no variation to this date and no extension.

In Unit 2, the date for the visiting **examiner** to come and assess your work will be arranged by your teacher. Except under exceptional circumstances, once the date has been fixed, it cannot be changed so the deadline is there for you to meet and to work towards.

This AS year, then, is about two units, and there is a lot of hard work ahead, but think about the rewards along the way and the skills you are going to develop alongside those people sitting in the room with you. We hope you will find the course enjoyable as well as rewarding and the challenges that you will face will equal anything else you will encounter in other areas of the curriculum. The top grades are there for the taking in a specification that recognises and rewards the contribution of the individual within the group.

There is no reason at all why you should not be aiming for an A* grade at the end of the course. You are going to have to work for it though – and the work starts here. Drama and Theatre Studies demands many different

examiner
The person who will come to apply the national standard to work presented for examination purposes.

things from students, and talent alone is not enough to see you through. We have never yet come across a student who didn't tell us they would like a Grade A or an A* at the end of the two year course.

If you are prepared to work at it and really want a chance of achieving a higher grade, then the extension material and homework activities will really help you to develop your work. In line with the aims of the Young, Gifted and Talented Programme (YG&T), the extension activities offer more advanced tasks to raise standards and to give you access to formal and informal opportunities to help you convert your potential into high achievement. You can find out more about YG&T at http://ygt.dcsf.gov.uk/Home Page.aspx?stakeholder=14.

EXTENSION MATERIAL AND HOMEWORK ACTIVITIES

Throughout the textbook, there are shaded boxes to illustrate particular points. Whenever you see one of these boxes, there will be a task that you may wish to follow up. Remember that this is your AS level course. Your teacher will be there to guide you in lesson times, but there is so much more that you can do to develop your studies and, of course, gain a higher grade.

The shaded boxes will usually offer extension material or homework activities and represent an invitation for you to get involved. They are only suggestions; as you work through the book, you may think of other related activities that could help you to increase your subject knowledge. Our intention is to point you in the right direction in a generic way; your response will need to explore in more detail the information we present here.

If you want a higher grade, we strongly recommend that you explore the information in the boxes, ideally for homework or in your free time.

PRACTICAL EXERCISES

improvising
Exploring character and situation to gain a greater understanding of the who, why and where of the relationships. Sometimes leads to performance but often used as a means of supporting more developed work around scripts.

Drama is a practical subject, and the best way to understand it is both to see live theatre and to actively participate in it. Practical drama lies at the heart of Units 1 and 2, and there is no better way to explore texts or to prepare for performance than to be up on your feet and **improvising**, rehearsing or trying out ideas to support the production process. As you start this course, you may already have decided that you are a performer, but don't let this stop you trying out a range of other practical activities, for example, having a go at costume design or directing a scene. Similarly, you may feel that your main interest is in technical theatre, but, likewise, to experience the play from the actor's point of view will enhance your overall understanding of the process.

Never spend too long discussing whether something will work or not, explore your ideas practically, the answer will become obvious.

WRITTEN EXERCISES AND THE QUALITY OF WRITTEN COMMUNICATION

The quality of written communication is very important and it is assessed to varying degrees across all of the units of this specification but particularly in Unit 1 and Unit 4. If you write regularly throughout the course, it will make a real difference to your ability to write well in both your coursework and the written aspects of the examinations, including the written element of Unit 2. The quality of your written communication has to be taken into account, and this is not simply a case of being able to spell the drama words correctly, it is more than that, it is also about the way you express yourself on the page in the context of the material you are being asked to write. There are word limits in place for all of the coursework in this specification, in the same way as there are time limits for performance work. You really need to be aware of how important this could be to your eventual marks, so it is a good idea to switch on to this now. By recognising the need to write clearly and concisely and by being able to structure responses to practical drama that are evaluative and analytical, you are setting yourself an approach to written communication that will enable you to access the demands of all of the units, including Unit 4 at the end of the A2 year.

Okay, just to get you into our way of working, we are now going to give you an extension activity to have a look at. This activity is typical of the type of thing you will find throughout the textbook and it should challenge but not baffle you. Look at the photograph that follows and consider the extension activity that goes with it.

Figure 2.1

Students exploring the theme of witchcraft.

Source: Alan Perks and Jacqueline Porteous

Extension Activity

Written response to an image

Consider Figure 2.1 and write three sentences that summarise the characters in situation as presented here. Your response must be detailed. Who are these characters and what do you think is happening based on the information in the picture? In a final sentence, evaluate the use of levels to indicate status in the photograph.

For each of the units, you will need a notebook that you can use as a working diary to record activities, your feelings about them and the learning experience you have been involved in.

You should get used to writing about what you do, what other people do, reflecting on your own work and that of others in the class and at the theatre. The reflection on the experience is important, developing your critical faculties in ways that will help you to access the higher level of marks for your written communication. It is not enough at this level of study to 'tell us about', you need to develop the capacity to 'tell us about and reflect upon', offering critical evaluation of your work and that of others. Part of this process is also about considering what else you could have seen or done; in other words, some alternatives, as there are always other ways of approaching things in the theatre.

Have a look at the sample diary extract that follows. This is one way of presenting the information. You may have a way that you think is more appropriate for your own notes. The extract will give you some idea of the kinds of things you may write in there and suggested approaches that may work for you. The important thing is that you see the notebook as a diary, as this will help you to write in the first person and to be more reflective of the process and your contribution to the activity.

SAMPLE DIARY EXTRACT, UNIT 1 EXPLORATION

Play One: *The House of Bernarda Alba* by Federico García Lorca

Date: 30 October 2009

In the lesson today, we were looking at some of the ideas of Stanislavsky. For home-work, we had to read pages 1–13 in a book called *Stanislavski and the Actor* by Jean Benedetti.

I was most interested by the notion of applying my **emotional memory** to a situation. We tried to apply this to the extract in the play when Bernarda is really sharp with Poncia. As I was playing Poncia, the servant, I tried to remember what is what like when we had someone really bossy at work (I'm a waitress at weekends) who ordered me around and never said please or thank you.

Because I found this quite difficult, we decided to do an improvisation of the scene at work, then try the extract from the play. I was delighted with the difference it made: both our characters, Poncia and Bernarda, seemed more realistic, and there was a real bitterness between the two of them that came out in our voices and our looks at each other.

emotion memory
Stanislavskian rehearsal technique in which actors are encouraged to draw on past experiences to help develop their relationship with their character.

Often, at the start of the course, your teacher will prompt you into recording information in your notebook but, before long, you will find that you do it automatically – and it is a useful habit to be getting into for other subjects too! In compiling your diary for this course, it is never enough to write what you did or what somebody else did. It is really good to get into the routine of giving your opinion about the work and reflecting upon it in a critical way. Two key words to bear in mind are 'analyse' and 'evaluate'. You will read more about these two words as you go through this textbook, and you will hear more about them from your teacher.

Do not postpone written work; it will be much more difficult to try to remember it later than tackling it straight away. Good-quality writing has a freshness and personal tone to it that tells the examiner or **moderator** that you have been involved with the activity and have understood it clearly. It should also demonstrate an understanding of the language of drama. Your notebook or diary is a great way of getting yourself into the habit of writing and reflecting as you go along.

'Analyse' means that you write objectively about something, explaining it by breaking it down into sections, supporting your opinion with 'why' and 'how'. 'Evaluate' means that you offer a balanced opinion, looking at

moderator
The person appointed by the Examination Board to ensure that work from your centre has been marked in line with the national standard.

something from both sides and justifying your conclusions. Both words mean that you are offering an opinion.

THE LANGUAGE OF DRAMA

Drama and Theatre Studies uses specialist phrases and terms. You should always use the language of drama when it is appropriate to do so whether you are speaking or writing. When you reach Unit 4, part of the assessment of your written communication will be based on your use of appropriate drama and theatre terminology. The more familiar you are with words and phrases – and their spelling – the more you will be able to demonstrate your understanding in your written work. The two units of the AS year are really useful for getting to grips with drama words and phrases and exploring them in a new context. There is an emphasis across the specification as a whole in the quality of your written communication which is taken into account in the awarding of marks, so it is a good idea for you to be on the ball right from the start of the course. Some words and phrases will come more naturally to you than others and will be more familiar to you through usage, particularly for those of you who have followed a GCSE drama course. For all of us, though, there really should be no excuse for misspelling words such as 'rehearsal', 'improvisation', 'character', particularly as these words are frequently spoken in this course and should almost as frequently be written down. If you are not sure how to spell something, then you must ask. You will probably find that others are sitting there around you wishing they had asked too – and are really pleased that you did!

> There is no shame in not knowing something; the shame is in not finding out when you realise that you don't.

Another thing that this textbook will do is to highlight and define specialist terms as they arise, and, once you have understood their meaning, you should make use of the language. Once you have understood the specialist term or word, the writing of it in context is usually enough to indicate that you have understood it, making it unnecessary to explain what a dramatic term means within the body of your written work.

A common mistake is to write something like this: 'at this point my character was hot-seated; hot-seating is when the other people working with you ask your character lots of questions in order to help you and them gain a better understanding of who you are.' You can always assume that the audience for your written work already knows and understands the language of drama.

There is a glossary at the end of the book that explains a range of terms. Try to know what all of these mean by the end of the AS year. In fact, start now.

Extension Activity

The language of drama and theatre

And the meaning is? Using the glossary find out the meaning of the following and write a sentence for each in your notebook to demonstrate your understanding.

1. Role
2. Improvising
3. Brechtian
4. Fourth Wall
5. Theatre of Cruelty

3 Theatrical timeline

Drama and Theatre Studies is such an exciting, vital and expanding world that there is always something new to learn. Your teacher will introduce you to new plays, playwrights, genres, practitioners and much more.

Greek drama began approximately 2,500 years ago, so already there is all that theatre history to explore. And, thinking ahead to the A2 year and Unit 4, some background knowledge of Greek theatre could prove very useful. See what you can find out about the Dionysus theatre. You should be able to gather a lot of information just by looking at Figure 3.1.

A basic knowledge of theatre history will really help you to put your work into a broad historical context. The timeline produced on pages 13–15 gives an overview of the past 2,000 plus years. A number of the major theatrical developments are outlined in the timeline, but, like everything else we offer you in this book, it is not the whole story. There are gaps here for you to fill in, and these will depend a great deal on the texts and practitioners your teacher chooses to study with you for Unit 1 and the choices you will make for performance texts for Unit 2.

Figure 3.1
Dionysus theatre.

Source: Joseph Kurchner (ed.)
The German 1891 Encyclopaedia,
Stuttgart: Deutsche
Verlagsgesellschaft.

Whenever a small 'c' is used, it is an abbreviation for the word 'circa' which means 'around'. In other words, the date is approximate, it is around the time specified.

GREEK THEATRE 2,400 YEARS AGO

525 BC – 456 BC	Aeschylus, *The Oresteia*
495 BC – 406 BC	Sophocles, *The Theban Plays, Antigone*
480 BC – 406 BC	Euripides, *The Trojan Women, The Bacchae*
456 BC – 386 BC	Aristophanes, *Lysistrata*

> *Lysistrata* is one of the possible set texts for Unit 4. Unless your teacher is certain that this play will not be studied for Unit 4, it is best *not* to study it for Unit 1 as you cannot use the same play for two different units. There is nothing to stop you reading it as part of your background research, of course.

1400	
1450	
1500	**MEDIEVAL THEATRE**
1564	William Shakespeare born in Stratford upon Avon

Mystery plays
Plays that tell the story of the Christian calendar, dated from around the fifteenth century.

Morality plays
Plays that had a strong moral content, that taught the audience something, e.g. *Everyman*.

ELIZABETHAN THEATRE

1576	The first Elizabethan playhouse opens
c.1580	Christopher Marlowe, *Doctor Faustus*
c.1592	Possibly the first performance of a Shakespeare play

> *Faustus* is one of the possible set texts for Unit 4. Unless your teacher is certain that this play will not be studied for Unit 4, it is best not to study it for Unit 1 as you cannot use the same play for two different units. There is nothing to stop you reading it as part of your background research, of course.

1600	
1612	John Webster, *The White Devil*
1642–1660	Theatres in England closed due to the Civil War
1675	William Wycherley, *The Country Wife*

Elizabethan theatre
From the time period of Queen Elizabeth I – usually associated with Shakespeare and Marlowe, but other influential playwrights were also at work during this period.

1700	George Farquhar, *The Recruiting Officer*
1706	
1775	Richard Brinsley Sheridan, *The Rivals*
1800	
1837–1879	Georg Buchner, *Woyzeck*

> *Woyzeck* is one of the possible set texts for Unit 4. Unless your teacher is certain that this play will not be studied for Unit 4, it is best not to study it for Unit 1 as you cannot use the same play for two different Units. There is nothing to stop you reading it as part of your background research, of course.

NINETEENTH-CENTURY THEATRE (150 YEARS AGO)

1879	Henrik Ibsen, *A Doll's House*
1890	Henrik Ibsen, *Hedda Gabler*
1895	Oscar Wilde, *The Importance of Being Earnest*
1896	Anton Chekov, *The Seagull*

1900 TWENTIETH-CENTURY THEATRE (100 YEARS AGO)

1912	George Bernard Shaw, *Pygmalion*
1923	George Bernard Shaw, *Saint Joan*
1939/40	Bertolt Brecht, *Mother Courage and Her Children*
1945	J. B. Priestley, *An Inspector Calls*
1949	Arthur Miller, *Death of a Salesman, A View from the Bridge, The Crucible*
1955	Tennessee Williams, *Cat on a Hot Tin Roof, The Rose Tattoo, The Glass Menagerie*
1956	John Osborne, *Look Back in Anger, The Entertainer*
1958	Shelagh Delaney, *A Taste of Honey*
1963	Joan Littlewood, *Oh! What a Lovely War*
1965	Joe Orton, *Loot*
	Edward Bond, *Saved*
1966	Tom Stoppard, *Rosencrantz and Guildenstern Are Dead*
1969	Steven Berkoff, *Metamorphosis*
1973	Peter Shaffer, *Equus*
	Athol Fugard, *The Island*
1974	Alan Ayckbourn, *Absent Friends*
	John McGrath, *The Cheviot, the Stag and . . .*
1977	Mike Leigh, *Abigail's Party*
1982	Caryl Churchill, *Top Girls*
1986	Jim Cartwright, *Road*
1992	Tony Kushner, *Angels in America*
1995	David Hare, *Skylight*
1997	Patrick Marber, *Dealer's Choice*
1999	Richard Norton-Taylor, *The Colour of Justice*

TWENTY-FIRST CENTURY THEATRE, MODERN TIMES

2000	Sarah Kane, *4:48 Psychosis*
	Joe Penhall, *Blue/Orange*
2003	Liz Lochhead, *Thebans*
	Martin McDonough, *The Pillowman*
2004	Alan Bennett, *The History Boys*
	David Eldridge, *Festen*
2007	David Hare, *The Permanent Way*
	Gregory Burke, *Black Watch*
2008	Polly Stenham, *That Face*
	Yasmina Reza, *God of Carnage*
	Tony Harrison, *Fram*

Extension Activity

Theatrical timeline

- Create your own theatrical timeline over the past 2,000-plus years using different plays to the ones listed above.
- Find other plays written by these well-known playwrights listed in this timeline.

Extension Activity

Read and compare

Modernising a play is a challenge as the author must always respect the original playwright's intentions so that the original is clearly evident in the updated version but so that it has a more contemporary feel to it.

- Compare *Antigone,* written approximately 2,400 years ago by Sophocles, with *Antigone* by Jean Anouilh (1944) or *Antigone* by Bertolt Brecht (1948).
- Compare *Medea* by Euripides with *Medea* by Liz Lochhead (2000).

Throughout this textbook, you will see reminders of when you could further your own knowledge of a particular person, event or theatrical element. In order for you to be able to make good use of this textbook, you need to see this as an opportunity to learn something new. You will almost certainly be able to connect any extended learning experience back to your own work.

4 Two golden rules

It is probably worth noting two of the golden rules of AS Drama and Theatre Studies at this point:

1. DEADLINES ARE DEADLINES ARE DEADLINES

If your teacher gives you a deadline for either written or practical work, then it is your job to meet that deadline. It is usually given in good time to allow your teacher to respond to your work before it has to be recorded or submitted to the Exam Board. The May deadline for Unit 1, for example, is for your teacher to submit work to the Exam Board. This means that your teacher will need it well in advance of his or her deadline in order to assess it before submitting it. Whether there are nine of you or thirty-nine of you in your group, this process will take time, and your teacher will want to give it his or her full attention in order to make sure you get the best possible mark for your efforts. It is very much in your interests to keep up with deadlines.

2. THE WORD LIMITS ON ANY WRITTEN WORK YOU SUBMIT ARE MAXIMUM LIMITS

The Exam Board has stated that there will be no tolerance here, so there is no point in doubling the word count in the hope of doubling your marks. It does not work like that. Anything over the published maximum number of words will be ignored by the teacher-assessor and by the moderator. Similarly, anything over the time limit for practical performances in Unit 2 will be ignored by your visiting examiner.

Keeping a word count

The easy way to keep a track of the number of words you have written is to use the word-count facility on your computer. Select the tab marked tools and click on the word count. This will then tell you the number of words you have used so far (see Figure 4.1). A lot of people leave word count activated all of the time as it is really useful for making sure that coursework is of the required length. It is good practice to work to a word limit as it is probably important for all of your subjects at this level of study.

Figure 4.1
Use the word-count facility on your computer.

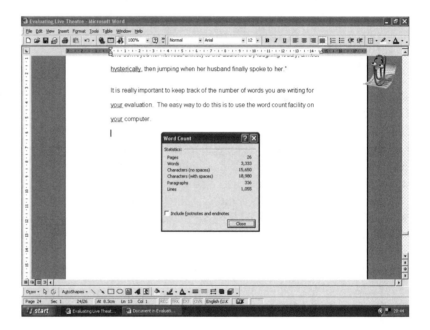

5 Who are they? Examiners and moderators unmasked

Although it may seem a little premature to go into details about examinations when you are only just setting out on the course, it might be worth putting the process into context for you right at the start of your AS year.

Your teacher is your assessor for Unit 1, and the work is moderated. Your contribution to Unit 2 is assessed by an examiner.

It is probably a good idea to have a look at who these people are and what impact they can have on your final results. We will assume that you have already met your teacher so the following will put the work for you and your teacher into the framework of the examination.

THE EXAMINER

The Examiner is appointed by the Examination Board to carry out duties in relation to the externally assessed components of the specification, in this case Unit 2 and, in the A2 year, Unit 4.

The Examiner is or has been a teacher, with the vast majority of examiners currently teaching the specification – ask your teacher, he or she may be an examiner.

Examiners are trained every year to help them to apply the agreed standard to their work in centres, and it is compulsory for examiners to attend a standardisation meeting before they are allowed to visit centres or mark exam papers. The standardisation meetings are organised by the Examination Board and led by the Principal Examiner – the person who is responsible for ensuring the standard of marking is maintained from year to year in that unit. You may find yourself performing your Unit 2 pieces in front of a 'panel' of examiners. This panel could consist of:

- your examiner
- your examiner's team leader

- an assistant principal examiner
- the Principal Examiner for Unit 2
- the Chief Examiner for the specification.

First, DON'T PANIC! It is very rare for there to be a panel of five examiners – but it could happen. The important thing to remember is that there is only one person there to look at your work, and that is your examiner; the others are there to ensure that the standard of the examination is being maintained, and this is part of the process. If your examiner is going to have an accompanied visit – which could just be a team leader – then he or she will know in advance and will let your teacher know so you will be aware of this before the day. It will not in any way affect your performances: you just go ahead as normal.

THE MODERATOR

The Moderator is appointed by the Examination Board to carry out moderation of the internally assessed components of the specification. In Drama and Theatre Studies, this means Unit 1 and, in the A2 year, Unit 3. The Moderator is or has been a teacher, with the vast majority of moderators currently teaching the specification. During your contribution to Unit 1, your teacher-assessor will make notes that will eventually help him or her to come to a decision about the marks you will be awarded for your contribution to the exploration process of both texts and your evaluation of the live theatre performance. At every stage of the process, your teacher-assessor is looking for opportunities to reward your work against the published criteria. Your teacher-assessor is not looking to penalise you for anything. At the end of the Unit 1 time period, your teacher-assessor will award you marks against the published criteria and submit these alongside a written summary of why you have been awarded those marks. The Moderator's job is then to look at the evidence submitted and decide whether or not the mark you have been given reflects marks for work of a comparable standard across the country. If it does, then your teacher-assessor's mark will stand. If it does not, then the moderator has the job of adjusting the mark to bring it in line with the national standard. In some circumstances, the moderator may request further evidence of work from your teacher-assessor, so it is really important that all of your work is kept safe and secure until the very end of the moderation process.

SUMMARY OF THE PROCESS FOR EXAMINERS AND MODERATORS

- An examiner will mark your work.
- A moderator does not mark your work but checks the marking already done by your teacher as assessor.
- Many examiners are also moderators, and many teachers are moderators and examiners.
- Examiners and moderators meet on a regular basis – either in person or electronically – in order to ensure that a standard is maintained throughout the examination series, and each specification has a chief examiner who has an overview of all of the individual units and is the ultimate connection between the examining teams and the subject officers or assessment leaders within the examination boards.

Have a look at Edexcel's website at www.edexcel.org.uk. You will probably be surprised at the size of the organisation and the range of qualifications and other services offered.

6 A final few words before you get started

Drama is essentially a creative subject that relies heavily on your imagination and experiences. Inevitably, the examination process can be seen as confining that creativity. However, what examination drama does give is credibility to a subject which has been around in schools as an educational medium for over fifty years but which has sometimes been seen as something of a 'Cinderella' subject in terms of funding and recognition. This is changing rapidly in the current climate as drama is becoming recognised by employers as one of the most useful subjects to have, be it at A Level or degree level. The extract below is taken from a recent edition of the University of Central Lancashire's prospectus:

> There are many careers which are open to Drama and Theatre Studies students including management, personnel and social work, team management and jobs requiring analytical and presentational skills. Popular career destinations include teaching and careers in the theatre or the media. Taking Drama and Theatre Studies will equip you with some important skills for your future career. Two of the qualities most valued by employers in applicants are literacy and creativity. Drama and Theatre Studies will demonstrate that you can work productively as part of a team and that you can demonstrate initiative and imagination in creating new opportunities.

You can be reassured that Edexcel's Drama and Theatre Studies specifications have gained a fantastic reputation over the years with both higher-education providers and potential employers. There is real anecdotal evidence of this (ask your teacher), but there is also hard evidence from real people – people just like you – entering university or employment and effectively using their Drama and Theatre Studies-related skills to develop and enhance future learning. It may seem at times that you are spending a lot of time jumping through exam-related hoops instead of creatively exploring exciting aspects of theatre and performance. Hopefully, there will be a balance of activity that your teacher will be able to maintain with you, but, in order to be able to access the wider theatrical world – if that is your intention upon completing this course – then you must recognise the structures that need to be in place to help you to develop your understanding.

The truth is that everything we do is measured by qualifications, and what better qualification to have than an A Level in Drama and Theatre Studies? Onwards, then, but with one eye firmly on the deadlines your teacher will set for you while the other is on the costume cupboard just in case you do get the chance to escape occasionally into another character in another world.

UNIT 1
EXPLORATION
OF DRAMA AND
THEATRE

PART II

7 Overview of Unit 1

This unit offers you the chance to demonstrate your skills in exploring two contrasting play texts chosen by your teacher, in a practical and active way. Here are the Assessment Objectives for Unit 1. These are the targets that you are measured against, in other words it is how well you do these things that counts.

ASSESSMENT OBJECTIVES FOR UNIT 1

- **AO2** (15 per cent): Demonstrate knowledge and understanding of practical and theoretical aspects of drama and theatre using appropriate terminology.
- **AO4** (5 per cent): Make critical and evaluative judgements of live theatre.

You will cover a minimum of two play texts in this unit and explore both in their theatrical context. You will also have the opportunity of seeing a live theatre production, which you have to review. This may be a production of one of the two play texts you are exploring, but it does not have to be.

At least one of these plays must be explored in the light of a recognised theatre practitioner. A theatre practitioner is someone who has had a significant influence on theatre styles, for example, Konstantin Stanislavsky, Bertolt Brecht or Antonin Artaud. A practitioner may also be a theatre company who have made an impression with their own unique style, for example, Théâtre de Complicité or Kneehigh Theatre Company.

You will also be introduced to the written elements of the course as part of the induction, and it is essential that you recognise the importance of the quality of written communication right from the start of the AS year. All units lead towards Unit 4, the final written examination in the A2 year. This unit (Unit 4) is worth 30 per cent of the total A Level mark, and, therefore, any opportunity your teacher gives you to write across all of the units should be seized upon straight away.

Unit 1 is called 'Exploration of Drama and Theatre', and there certainly are a lot of practical activities in this unit, but alongside these, there is a requirement for you to be able to reflect upon your experience in a structured written way.

The knowledge and understanding you will gain through the study of the two or three plays in this unit will develop and grow with you as you prepare for Unit 2. The exploration is not just about the texts, it is also about developing explorative strategies that can be applied to any play text in any context.

The guided learning time for Unit 1 is around seventy hours to ninety hours, but that is just that: a guide. There will be times when you will need to do an extra workshop session during lunchtime or at the end of the day. It is very likely that homework will be set on a regular basis, and the hours will soon mount up.

Drama is a time-consuming business, and successful students must be prepared to put the time in.

The specification is the actual course or syllabus that you have to fulfil in order to complete the course. All that is required of you in terms of areas to be studied, and how you will be assessed, are available on the website, and you can look up lots of other information that is similar to the grid in Figure 7.1. See what else you can find out at:

- http://www.edexcel.com/notices/Pages/issue2.aspx
- http://www1.edexcel.org.uk/especs/GCE_Drama/wrapper.html

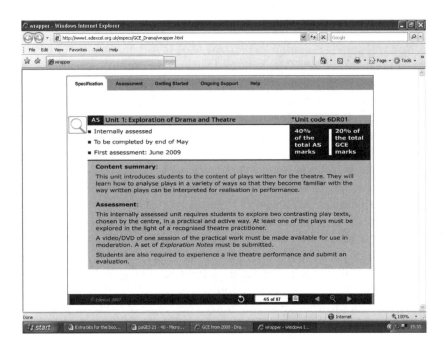

Figure 7.1

Unit 1, as described in the e-specification.

PRACTICAL EXPLORATION

Unit 1 is about getting up and getting on and finding ways of bringing the two plays to life in order for you to gain a greater understanding of the playwright's art and the text in relation to its rehearsal and performance opportunities. Almost all of your classroom and workshop time will be spent practically exploring the two plays. This will involve rehearsing scenes, directing scenes, trying out different **interpretations**, experimenting with staging, creating 'off-text' improvisations and other activities that will develop your understanding of the texts. As we have already mentioned, this will also help with your work on your Unit 2 texts and, looking forward to the A2 year, provide a real grounding in exploration that will help you enormously with your preparation for Unit 3 and Unit 4.

interpretation
The approach to a text a director will adopt to create a version of the play in performance that has a particular stamp on it. Look at the work of Katie Mitchell, for example.

EXPLORATION NOTES

Alongside the practical workshops which will be assessed by your teacher, you must submit written exploration notes that show how your practical work has led to an increased understanding of the plays. Your notes are worth up to 20 marks out of the 60 available for this unit, and, as we will detail as you go through this section of the book, the notes are your opportunity for reflecting on the practical experience and demonstrating your understanding of the exploration work you have been involved in.

EVALUATING A LIVE THEATRE PERFORMANCE

The final task for Unit 1 is to *evaluate* a live theatre performance. We have already mentioned that the play that you choose to evaluate *may* be one of the two plays you have explored practically for this unit *or* it may be a different play. Your teacher will decide whether you are going to study two or three texts for this unit. Your evaluation of a live theatre performance will be written and must not exceed 1,000 words maximum.

Use the Edexcel website to find out what it says in the specification about how practical exploration, exploration notes and evaluation of live theatre will be assessed.

CHOICE OF PLAYS

Your teacher will choose two plays which you are going to explore throughout Unit 1. The plays will offer you a suitable challenge so that you can achieve the higher band marks. Therefore, the plays should be more demanding than the texts you might have studied at GCSE. The Exam Board, also known as the Awarding Body, does not give a choice here: it is entirely up to your teacher to decide, and there are probably a range of reasons why particular texts may be chosen.

There are a couple of things your teacher will need to take into account in the choice. These are set out in the specification, but, within these parameters, there is freedom of choice. With freedom comes the responsibility your teacher has for ensuring as far as possible that the texts chosen not only meet the very clear criteria from the Exam Board but that they also allow you the opportunity to be able to access the marks through your practical exploration and written evaluation.

The plays your teacher chooses have to meet the following criteria:

- Each play must be by a different playwright.
- They must be by a known playwright, in other words, a playwright who is published and recognised. The play must have an ISBN number.
- At least one of the plays must be explored alongside a well-known theatre practitioner. For example, if one of the texts chosen by your teacher was *The Seagull* by Anton Chekhov, you would probably look at the Russian director Konstantin Stanislavsky. If you were doing a play by Sarah Kane, you would probably look at this play in relation to the influence of Antonin Artaud.

For example

1. Play A: *Death of a Salesman* by Arthur Miller.
2. Play B: *Mother Courage* by Bertolt Brecht.
3. Play C: *Equus* by Peter Schaffer.

Taking the three plays above, your teacher could use them to complete Unit 1 in the following way:

Table 7.1 *Possible combinations of plays for Unit 1.*

Explore Play A	Explore Play A
Explore Play B	Explore Play B
Evaluate a production of Play A	Evaluate a production of Play C
Two plays studied	Three plays studied

UNIT 1: TWO OR THREE PLAYS?

For Unit 1, you could use two plays as a minimum, or three plays as a maximum if your evaluation of a live performance is on a different play (this would then be your third play).

The advantage of studying two plays is that you need a working knowledge of only two texts. This *may* allow you to study in greater depth and detail. This option could be preferable if you were short of time.

The advantage of studying three plays is that it increases your knowledge, and you may be glad of a change of text. Although you cannot use these exact texts anywhere else in the course, it is possible that you will have gained a really firm grasp of three different genres. Similarly, you might choose a play text for Unit 2 that is by one of the *playwrights* studied for Unit 1. These links will become increasingly useful to you as you progress through the course.

MAKING DECISIONS

In Unit 1, your teacher will make decisions about the choice of texts and the appropriate practitioner or practitioners to be studied. Different routes to the same destination might be:

Route 1

- *All My Sons* by Arthur Miller, 1947.
- *The Three Sisters* by Anton Chekhov, 1901. (Practitioner: Konstantin Stanislavsky.)
- Evaluation of a performance: *Lear* by Edward Bond, 1971.

Route 2

- *Blood Wedding* by Federico Garcia Lorca, 1932.
- *Mother Courage* by Bertolt Brecht, 1939. (Practitioner: Bertolt Brecht.)
- Evaluation of a performance: *The Resistible Rise of Arturo Ui* by Bertolt Brecht, 1941.

Route 3

- *Vincent in Brixton* by Nicholas Wright, 2002.
- *The Marat Sade* by Peter Weiss, 1963. (Practitioner: Antonin Artaud.)
- Evaluation of a performance: *The Marat Sade* by Peter Weiss, 1963.

Route 4

- *Stuff Happens* by David Hare, 2004.
- *A Midsummer Night's Dream* by William Shakespeare, 1595. (Practitioner: Peter Brook.)
- Evaluation of a performance: *Frost/Nixon* by Peter Morgan, 2006.

Route 5

- *Fences* by August Wilson, 1955
- *Cat on a Hot Tin Roof* by Tennessee Williams, 1955. (Practitioner: Konstantin Stanislavsky.)
- Evaluation of a performance: *Who's Afraid of Virginia Woolf?* by Edward Albee, 1962.

How many of these plays listed above have you:

- heard of?
- read?
- seen in performance?

Extension Activity

Play-reading exercise

Choose one play from each of the alternative routes above and set yourself the task to read all five plays during the first term of the course. You should then write an evaluation of each of the plays of no more than 500 words in your notebook:

- What did you think of it?
- Why did you think that?
- How might you stage the play in performance?

8 Practical exploration

You will find from talking to friends and from your own experience in other subjects that most courses begin with some kind of induction. In Drama and Theatre Studies, this could probably take a few weeks where your drama group will get to know each other better. Typically, you will do lots of practical activities that will allow you to move forward as a group. Practical drama is at the heart of this specification, and it is through exploring drama and theatre by improvising, rehearsing and performing that you will be best placed to complete the necessary written work with clarity and under-standing.

Drama teachers have a saying that plays aren't meant to be read, they should be performed, staged or directed. Many people discuss the countless ways there are to get a play from page to stage. Whatever route you choose, plays are about getting up and exploring the many creative options available to you whatever your area of expertise. So, this section of the book is full of ideas to help you and to encourage you practically:

* How to explore a play.
* Reading the play.
* Annotating the play.

HOW TO EXPLORE A PLAY

Unit 1 should give you a really firm foundation for the rest of the course. You should feel confident about how plays are structured, the circumstances that are relevant to each particular play, and how the play could be staged.

You need to do as much practical work as possible on both of the plays chosen for exploration.

READING THE PLAY

This sounds obvious, but reading the entire play as quickly as possible will free your time up to concentrate on more detailed issues. The essence of this as stated above is how might you stage the play once you've read it. The running time of an average play is around two to three hours, but you should be able to read it in half that time. This would be a good early homework activity.

Your teacher may choose to read it with you aloud in class, which can also be very useful. Some directors choose to spend a considerable amount of time reading the play until every member of the company is certain what everything means. This can take up a lot of time, but, depending on the choice of play, it may be time well spent. It is certainly much easier to read a play out loud so you can 'hear' it, and, if it doesn't feel too silly, you can even read it out loud to yourself and have different voices for the different characters. This is also an exercise you can do in your head if you are reading it on your own, either for homework, or simply for pleasure.

ANNOTATING THE PLAY

Annotating a play that you are working on is a habit you should get into straight away. A sharp HB pencil should accompany your text at all times. If you don't know what something means in a play, be it a word or a phrase, you cannot communicate effectively with your audience. By writing notes alongside the text, you are developing your understanding of the play. Every time you come across something you don't understand, didn't know, or your teacher points out to you, write it into your text for future reference. An example of an annotated text is given below.

Figure 8.1
Annotated text: *Measure for Measure*.

Here is an extract from Shakespeare's *Measure for Measure*

With the annotations added in GREY to illustrate the Director's/actor's intentions.

CLAUDIO

Now, sister, what's the comfort? He goes to her and takes her hands

ISABELLA

Why,
As all comforts are; most good, most good indeed.
Lord Angelo, having affairs to heaven,
Intends you for his swift ambassador,
Where you shall be an everlasting leiger:
Therefore your best appointment make with speed;
To-morrow you set on.

> **Said quite quickly, Isabella is really sentencing her brother to death, she must feel some sense of guilt and sadness.**

Figure 8.1
continued

CLAUDIO

Is there no remedy? Puzzled

ISABELLA

None, but such remedy as, to save a head,
To cleave a heart in twain.

> Isabella really believes
> that she cannot possibly
> save him. She must be
> resolute.

CLAUDIO

But is there any? Getting desperate

ISABELLA

Yes, brother, you may live:
There is a devilish mercy in the judge,
If you'll implore it, that will free your life,
But fetter you till death.

CLAUDIO

Perpetual durance? He doesn't understand

ISABELLA

Ay, just; perpetual durance, a restraint,
Though all the world's vastidity you had,
To a determined scope.

CLAUDIO

But in what nature? Tell me more...

ISABELLA

In such a one as, you consenting to't,
Would bark your honour from that trunk you bear,
And leave you naked.

CLAUDIO

Let me know the point. Getting frustrated with her

ISABELLA

O, I do fear thee, Claudio; and I quake,
Lest thou a feverous life shouldst entertain,
And six or seven winters more respect
Than a perpetual honour. Darest thou die?
The sense of death is most in apprehension;
And the poor beetle, that we tread upon,
In corporal sufferance finds a pang as great
As when a giant dies.

> She's stalling him.
> She sees that he may not
> accept her reason or
> believe in the things she
> thinks are important.

PRACTICAL EXPLORATION

Practical exploration is the key to success on this unit. Your teacher will have lots of practical activities to support your chosen texts, but typical practical activities could be as follows:

- improvising scenes
- off-text improvisation
- still image work
- interpreting text.

Improvising scenes

It can be difficult to explore a scene from a play when you have the text in your hand trying to read the words and do the scene justice. As long as you respect the playwright's intentions and try to keep as close as you can to the sentiments of the scene, improvising it in your own words can be very illuminating. Students are often surprised by just how many of the play-wright's words do come back to them, although this is not as important as understanding the basic meaning of the scene. In other words, as soon as you have understood the basic **plot** and gist of a scene, you put the script down, and do it in your own words.

plot
The story of the drama – what happens to who and why.

Off-text improvisation

This requires more imagination than improvising scenes from the text as you are focusing on a scene or scenes that the playwright didn't script. This is often something that took place before the play begins, a scene that might take place after the play has ended or a scene that is referred to in the text but the audience don't actually see. For example, if you were exploring *Romeo and Juliet* by William Shakespeare, you could improvise a scene before the play begins. This could be a scene with Juliet's father saying that she must keep away from the Montague family, and, in particular, their young son, Romeo. We don't know how accurate a scene like this might be, but it can be really beneficial when it comes to understanding how characters develop, as well as some of their 'backstory'.

Still image work

Capturing a scene or a unit of the play in a still image can be a particularly useful exercise. Your teacher might ask you to sum up all of Act I in four still images. This exercise will force you to be highly selective and focus only on the things that really matter, the key moments. This can lead to some excellent discussion work from the rest of your group who may have chosen different moments to you. Similarly, they may have chosen the same moments, and this also leads to valid discussion points.

Interpreting text

It's not always what we say, but how we say it! Tone of voice, emphasis on particular words, use of pauses can all affect the meaning of words. It is not difficult to show that Hamlet is mad if some of the things he says are delivered in a wild and frenzied tone. It is just as possible to say the same words in a different way, interpreted to show that he is depressed and sad. Directors have always relied heavily on interpretation to communicate their meaning to an audience.

Extension Activity

The opening scene from *A View from the Bridge*

An excellent play script to look at to understand how text can be misinterpreted is *A View from the Bridge* by Arthur Miller. In the opening scenes, look at the relationship between Eddie and Catherine. You will see that it is quite possible to misconstrue their relationship depending on how the words are said, where Eddie and Catherine are when they are speaking to each other, and how close they are to each other.

MOVEMENT AND PROXEMICS

Figure 8.2 shows that the actors' positioning on the stage is crucial, and, without even knowing the play that is being performed, we can glean much information from this image. The two actors facing us are clearly united in their attack on the girl with the plait in her hair. They are raised slightly higher than her, which increases their status and their superiority. Finally,

proxemics
Establishing relationships between actors and between actors and audience through exploring stage positioning and usually defined during the blocking process of rehearsal.

Figure 8.2
Movement and proxemics: the distance between characters when they are onstage can communicate a great deal to the audience.

Source: Alan Perks and Jacqueline Porteous.

their expression towards her shows aggression and displeasure, all of which highlight her vulnerability.

It is possible to communicate a great deal without even speaking, and we call this non-verbal language. For example, we can usually tell if someone is angry with us as they approach us because their movement, expressions and gestures will all be communicating this to us before they even speak. It can be useful to explore a scene 'silent movie' style, as this will really make you work hard at exaggerating your actions, and all movement will have to communicate something. Although this style can appear quite ridiculous, it does serve a purpose in helping you to select appropriate movements for each scene.

The proxemics of a scene are important to explore because they can illustrate status and intention and can provide an insight to the characters. They also have a bearing on the stage space to be used.

DIRECTING A SCENE

Directing a scene from a play really places the responsibility for what is communicated and how decisions are made firmly on your shoulders. It is a really exciting position to be in and one which all students should attempt at least once during the AS year. While it is sensible to work collaboratively with your peers as you direct them, it is possibly the best way to understand how text can be interpreted and communicated effectively to your audience. Whenever your teacher puts you in groups, if there is someone left over, volunteer to do some directing work as you will learn much from the process.

PERFORMING AN EXTRACT

It is not a requirement for Unit 1 that you have to present a polished performance of any part of the plays explored. Performance work is very time-consuming, and it is possible to successfully complete all your practical work, which is coursework, in normal workshop and classroom conditions.

However, some students may wish to conclude the unit with some practical work which is more formal if this seems a logical extension of the work that you have done. This could then play a part in your supporting notes, although it would *not* be appropriate to include a polished performance on the video/DVD that your centre has to submit to the Exam Board. This is just another idea for exploring the text. It may, of course, prove useful for Unit 2, as you are improving your performance skills.

HOW MUCH HELP CAN YOUR TEACHER GIVE YOU?

The practical workshops and lessons will be led primarily by your teacher. You are at the start of a new course, and their knowledge and expertise is key to your success. It is quite likely that as you progress through this unit you will assume more scope and responsibility for the practical sessions. Remember that the more you are actively involved in exploring the texts, the more you will learn. Your teacher will help you to structure your notes and will almost certainly suggest areas for improvement, but there is a fine balance to be struck with coursework as to how much help you can have before the work is no longer seen as your own. Your teacher will help you, but you will also have to help yourself. Your teacher is your examiner for this Unit and must therefore maintain an appropriate balance between guiding you and doing the work for you. There must be real integrity on the part of your teacher in ensuring that there is a fair distribution of necessary information during the exploration process and that you all have access to knowledge to develop your understanding in order for you to be able to produce the written elements to the best of your ability.

Extension Activity

Presentation to the rest of your drama group

You could offer to do a presentation to the rest of your group about any aspect that is referred to in lesson time that you would like to know more about. This could be about one of the practitioners, or something about a playwright, or just to develop one small element that little bit further. This would not only develop everyone's knowledge, it would also give you more to refer to in your own exploration notes.

The real joy of practical work, indeed of Drama and Theatre Studies, is that there is so much to discover. Whenever students ask us a question, we encourage them to get up, try it out, and discover the answer for themselves. There are some things about a play that can never be changed. For example, it would be ridiculous to do *The Trojan Women* by Euripides as a comedy: clearly, this play, about the wars of Troy, is a **tragedy**. However, there are things in the play which are open to debate and interpretation. As a director, you may have ideas about how a scene might be played, but, until you actually try it out practically, you will never know the answer.

tragedy
A style of theatre stemming from Ancient Greece and developed through the centuries by playwrights, most famously Shakespeare, in which the protagonist or hero suffers serious misfortune, usually as a result of human and divine actions.

9 Exploration notes

EXPLORING THE PLAYS

Your teacher will choose two play texts for you to explore which will give you a firm foundation for the rest of the course. It is likely that you will spend equal amounts of time on each text to reflect the advice given in the specification.

Although you do not need to do a word count to see that you have written exactly the same number of words on each play, it is a good idea to try to keep them fairly even. Three thousand words is probably less than you think. You are going to write 3,000 words maximum, across *both* play texts. You may decide to write about each play separately, or you could write about both of them at the same time.

Figure 9.1
Play 1, followed by Play 2.

Alternatively, you may decide it suits your purposes and your style to write about both plays simultaneously, mixing and matching your ideas in response to particular aspects of both plays.

```
1 2 1 2 1 2 . . . .
. . . . 2 1 2 1 2 1 . . . .

Maximum 3,000 words

Key:  1 = Play 1
      2 = Play 2
```

Figure 9.2
Mixing both plays.

Your teacher will guide you on the format of your notes. You may find sub-headings useful, or you may prefer to write in a more traditional essay style. You don't have to have a title but, again, you may find it useful to have a focus for your notes. The specification indicates very clearly the areas that your notes should cover in relation to the texts explored. These areas could easily give appropriate divisions and headings to your work.

It is essential to note that in the specification it says you *must* cover these areas in your notes:

- language
- non-verbal language
- vocal awareness
- characterisation
- the social, cultural, historical and political context
- the visual, aural, and spatial elements of production
- the response to a practitioner
- interpretation.

Plus, of course, you need to include an evaluation of a live theatre performance, which is an additional 1,000 words (this is dealt with in detail in Chapter 10). As soon as you start to explore the plays practically, you need to start making your notes. Once you have done your research and specific practical exploration led by your teacher, you could use a working title for your notes such as:

- Show how your practical exploration of the two texts has developed your understanding of each playwright's intentions (3,000 words maximum).
- Give a detailed account of how your practical exploration of *All My Sons* by Arthur Miller enhanced your understanding of the play in production (1,500 words maximum).
- Using evidence from your practical workshops, analyse the production opportunities *Absurd Person Singular* by Alan Ayckbourn presents to the director and the designer (1,500 words maximum).
- In the light of your workshops on Bertolt Brecht, discuss the production opportunities presented by *The Caucasian Chalk Circle* by Bertolt Brecht (1,500 words maximum).

Of course, you do not have to have a title such as the ones above: you could do what we have suggested earlier and systematically use the suggested headings given in the specification and methodically go through the two plays.

In the following section, we have provided some possible ideas to further develop these elements in your written work, remembering that 3,000 words on the two texts in total does not leave you much room for manoeuvre.

LANGUAGE

While you must always remember that this is Drama and Theatre Studies and not English Literature, the language element is concerned with how the language of the play might be explored in performance. It refers to volume, tone, pace, accent and delivery. This is best referenced with your own practical exploration: for example: 'When I played the role of Dromio, I found that my voice was most effective when . . .'

Below are some useful questions that you might ask yourself when looking at the aspect of language. In this example, they refer to *A View from the Bridge* by Arthur Miller, but the questions could adapt instantly to suit any play.

- Where is the play set?
- What effect does this have on accent/dialect?
- Are there any Americanisms?
- Choice of vocabulary: Are certain words worthy of note? Have they become dated?
- Do some characters have catchphrases, use slang, overuse words, repeat themselves, swear, adopt a tone? If so, why?
- Is the language complex? Is it simple? Give examples.
- Is there use of metaphor, imagery, symbolism? (Take care to think practically, this would usually be an English Literature-type response.)
- Is the language heightened? Poetic? Emotive? Rhythmical? Hysterical? Contradictory? Give examples.
- Do the characters ask questions? Of whom?
- Use of pauses. Length of sentences. Length of speeches.
- Use of sub-text? Non-verbal language?
- What are the implications of these elements?
- Does the language communicate?
- What have you discovered about the language while you have been working on and exploring the text?
- Do you notice some differences in the language between the text, the stage play you might see and the film version? How does this compare to your own practical work in class?

The following pages contain some worked examples that address the questions asked above.

Using annotated text can be a quick and efficient way of showing how you have addressed the work practically. In the example given in Figure 9.3, the student has shown an excellent understanding of how the language functions. They have also shown excellent understanding and knowledge through their practical exploration of the play's language. This kind of activity

Figure 9.3

Annotated text: *A View from the Bridge.*

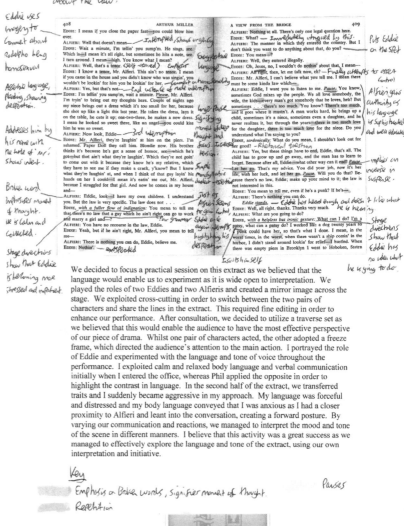

We decided to focus a practical session on this extract as we believed that the language would enable us to experiment as it is wide open to interpretation. We played the roles of two Eddies and two Alfieris and created a mirror image across the stage. We exploited cross-cutting in order to switch between the two pairs of characters and share the lines in the extract. This required fine editing in order to enhance our performance. After consultation, we decided to utilize a traverse set as we believed that this would enable the audience to have the most effective perspective of our piece of drama. Whilst one pair of characters acted, the other adopted a freeze frame, which directed the audience's attention to the main action. I portrayed the role of Eddie and experimented with the language and tone of voice throughout the performance. I exploited calm and relaxed body language and verbal communication initially when I entered the office, whereas Phil applied the opposite in order to highlight the contrast in language. In the second half of the extract, we transferred traits and I suddenly became aggressive in my approach. My language was forceful and distressed and my body language conveyed that I was anxious as I had a closer proximity to Alfieri and leant into the conversation, creating a forward posture. By varying our communication and reactions, we managed to interpret the mood and tone of the scene in different manners. I believe that this activity was a great success as we managed to effectively explore the language and tone of the extract, using our own interpretation and initiative.

is also worth considering when you come to compiling your rationale for Unit 2 Section A, as it really helps your examiner to gain an understanding of how much you have been able to respond practically to an extract to show your understanding of the playwright's intentions at that particular point.

WORKED EXAMPLE

The next worked example uses *Metamorphosis* by Steven Berkoff.

Metamorphosis: Use Of Language

A feature of language used frequently in Metamorphosis is choral repetition. In a group response to this we found that one can experiment with many different ways of delivering the repetition. I found that an effective method was to keep a monotonous tone, as this increased the persistent nature of the family's demands. It also shows the dull and hollow expectance they have of Gregor.

> 'Gregor! /
> Cash! /
> Gregor! /
> Shoes!'

Another dominant aspect of language used by Berkoff is non-verbal communication and mime. We found that when coupling the repetition with mime the effect was more profound. Berkoff intends this marriage of verbal and non-verbal communication in the stage directions. This tallies with his notion of Total Theatre, as the actors are relying on their physical capabilities to communicate. Often the mime engages the audience, drawing attention to otherwise insignificant details, through details that build the environment and atmosphere around the actor. I found that when performing a mime it was important to keep it simple and focus all your concentration on the act you are trying to portray. I discovered an effective approach was to focus intently on a specific detail, as I felt this gave the mime more credibility, and enhanced the illusion. For example, when miming drinking a mug of tea, I might decide to concentrate in my head on what pattern is on the mug. Your own belief in what you are doing aids the belief of the audience in what you are doing.

> (Family mime actions of domestic life in time to ticking, resembling those automatic figures in wax-works)

The overall tone of language in the play is harsh, often when the family speak regarding Gregor. Similarly, Gregor's tone is often distressed, initially at his condition but later at the burden he feels he has become on his family. Gregor's panic is shown through his short disjointed sentences. This forces his speech to speed up and therefore increases the distress or tension in his voice. The accompaniment of agitated actions in this extract creates an atmosphere of panic effectively. These acute styles of language, which dominate the play, create a tension that periodically builds as Gregor's condition depreciates. This tension is eventually released once Gregor finally dies. Then the family are able to communicate in a more relaxed tone.

> Gregor: Shut my eyes – I'm dreaming. (To his legs and arms as if wishing them to dissolve) Go Away! It's nonsense – it must go away – spots on my belly? Ooh!

> Mr S: Our Son! You can't call him our son any more – not that thing in there! Our son's left us.

Particularly, they talk to each other with affection for the first time. Another use of language is direct address, which significantly adds to the unrealistic stylised feel of the play. All the characters are able to come out of character and use this device in order to effectively narrate the story to the audience. I found this a very useful method in performance, as it enables Berkoff to save time telling the story and draw more focus to the characters themselves. It also is a useful tool to engage the audience and make them feel involved. This is noticeably effective at the very beginning of the play, as the characters present the play directly, immediately drawing the attentions of the audience in.

> Mrs S: My daughter has bloomed into a pretty girl.

> Mr S: As Gregor Samsa awoke one morning from uneasy dreams…
> Mrs S: He found himself transformed into a gigantic insect…

Figure 9.4
Worked example: *Metamorphosis*.

In the example used from *Metamorphosis,* note the number of times the student uses the word 'I'. She has put herself at the heart of the response. This work is not copied from a book or downloaded from the Internet: it reflects genuine learning and discovery from time spent exploring the play. However, the work already is at a word count of 474 words. It does cover some of the other areas suggested in the specification, for example, it refers to characterisation, non-verbal communication and vocal awareness, but you need to be careful in your own work that you have an eye very firmly on the upper word limit.

WORKED EXAMPLE

A different type of worked example from *A View From the Bridge* by Arthur Miller could be along the following lines:

> I feel that Eddie's tone after he meets Rodolpho is quite threatening, and you can sense that there is an element of jealousy as Eddie fears that Rodolpho may fancy Catherine. Catherine's body language is flirtatious as she runs her hands down her skirt. When playing the character of Catherine, I found her quite childish, particularly when she talks to Eddie. When I first read the play, I thought that Catherine was Eddie's girlfriend until their relationship became more clear. Looking at Eddie's body language in Act I when he is twisting the newspaper, you can see that he is tense. It may also imply that he feels aggression to Rodolpho or simply that he is threatened by him.

NON-VERBAL COMMUNICATION

This can be best illustrated by annotating a script extract. It can be as simple as pointing out where an actor should frown, raise an eyebrow or even sit down in order to communicate something to the audience that is done rather than said. This can also be an excellent section for you to talk about proxemics.

Proxemics means the distance, space or positioning between the actors and the audience at a given moment, for example, in *A Doll's House* by Henrik Ibsen, if the director wishes to show that Nora is flirting with Dr Rank, her words can take on greater or less significance depending on how close she is to him physically. In your exploration notes, this could read as:

We felt that the relationship between Nora and Dr Rank was utterly harmless so we made sure that we kept them apart when acting their scenes out. However, another group wished to suggest a sexual tension between them to give Nora more power so they made sure that the actors were always very close to each other. This familiarity and their use of proxemics made the audience slightly more sympathetic towards Helmer.

VOCAL AWARENESS

This is something that is easy to explore during practical workshops.

- What effect does it have when you use your voice in different ways?
- What effect does it have on the meaning of the words?
- What effect does it have on the audience?
- What effect does it have on your fellow actors?

You can try putting different emotions and feelings into the words you say, alter the volume, the pace, emphasise different words. This can also relate to interpretation. Some of the things you try out may seem ridiculous, but it is true that you can learn from your mistakes, so when you realise that something is wrong, it can confirm that another way it actually right.

Be brave about exploring different ideas, it is the only way to discover things for yourself.

CHARACTERISATION

This element can relate to language and interpretation. It is how you think a character should be played in performance. Do you imagine that he or she should be played as mean, selfish, devious, etc.? It is often about finding out his or her motive and purpose, which can be different depending on who they are speaking to.

WORKED EXAMPLE

A worked example to illustrate characterisation could be:

> My favourite character in *A View from the Bridge* by Arthur Miller is Beatrice. She is deceived by Eddie, and I found her the most challenging role to play in class. Miller gives very little away in his stage directions regarding Beatrice, so as a group we decided we wanted her to stand her ground against Eddie and to be strong. Perhaps her most significant line is: 'When will I be a wife again Eddie?' We tried this several different ways, with Beatrice challenging Eddie's masculinity to her almost apologising as she said it. I preferred it when Beatrice stood tall and looked Eddie in the eye. She was gentle with him but firm and I felt this was more what Miller wanted.

WORKED EXAMPLE

Here is a different worked example that looks at the character of Marco in the same play:

> When I was acting out the scene where Marco lifts the chair up high above his head, I felt it was necessary for me to play Marco as aggressive because I wanted to show him in a different light. This not only shocks Eddie but will give the audience something to consider. This allows Marco to show his power and strength, and I decided to do it in this way as it explored different ways of using the script to change the impact on the audience.

THE SOCIAL, CULTURAL, HISTORICAL AND POLITICAL CONTEXT OF A PRODUCTION

Playwrights are often social historians, and it is said that they hold a mirror up to society, so it is not surprising that many plays have a relevance and connection to what was happening in the world at the time they were written. Take care if the play was written about a different time period, for example, *An Inspector Calls* by J. B. Priestley was written in 1945 but set in 1912.

Priestley deliberately set his play in 1912 because the date represented an era when all was very different from the time he was writing. In 1912, rigid class and gender boundaries seemed to ensure that nothing would change. Yet, by 1945, most of those class and gender divisions had been breached. Priestley wanted to make the most of these changes. Through this play, he encourages people to seize the opportunity the end of the war had given them to build a better, more caring society.

WORKED EXAMPLE

The Crucible by Arthur Miller was written in 1953 but set in 1692. Miller used historical distancing to make a very strong political point about an event that was happening in America at the time. By writing a play about a similar event that occurred almost 300 years earlier, he raised great awareness. You can find out more about *The Crucible* by looking it up at the following website: http://www.stagework.org.

(Extract from BBC GCSE Bitesize website: http://www.bbc.co.uk/schools/gcsebitesize/drama)

These plays give you the opportunity to comment on what was happening at the time they were written and the time they were set. It would be very unusual to study a play that didn't have some social, cultural, historical or political relevance.

Below are some useful questions that you might ask yourself when looking at the aspect of the social, cultural, historical and political. In the worked example above, they refer to *The Crucible* by Arthur Miller but they could be adapted very easily to suit any play.

- What do you know about Arthur Miller that has a relevance to the play?
- What was happening when the play was written? In America? In Britain?
- When was the play set? Why?
- What is the play's history? Has it always had a good audience response?
- Does it have a political context and resonance?
- Why has the play a relevance today?
- Why do you think theatres are still keen to stage it?
- Can you find out anything about the directors of past productions?
- What does the play say to you?
- Do you think that the play will stand the test of time?

Use the stagework.org website to see if you can find any other social, cultural, historical or political references.

Extension Activity

Research on a website

Using the Stagework website, can you find out:

*   Who adapted Brecht's play *The Life of Galileo,* and what did he find challenging about this?
*   Why is the Aleithiometer the most important **prop** (property) in the play *His Dark Materials?*

properties or props
Small items that an actor will carry on stage in order to help define character for the audience. Usually includes set dressing too.

THE VISUAL, AURAL AND SPATIAL ASPECTS OF THE PRODUCTION

This is a speculative area that asks you to imagine that you are staging a production of the play you are exploring. It is always best to decide on a particular performance space which could be anything from a square box studio space to the London Palladium. As this is a theoretical question, you have no budget concerns or restraints, so it calls for an excellent working knowledge of the play, a good imagination, and off you go! How do you want your production of the play to *look* and *sound* on the stage of your choice? Below are some useful questions and phrases that you might ask yourself when looking at the aspect of visual, aural and spatial.

Visual, aural and spatial

This is a personal response, and you will gain higher marks if you keep relating your notes to your own practical work, for example:

*   When we discussed design concepts . . .
*   I liked the idea of . . .
*   In practical terms, this would/would not work . . .
*   It is important to use the playwright's descriptions because . . .
*   When we tried this scene in class we found that a chair was essential because . . .

Visual: What do want your audience to see?

- **set**
- staging used
- costume
- LFX
- use of colour
- props
- make-up
- symbols
- darkness and light
- images
- gauze
- **naturalistic** set
- non-naturalistic
- style

set
The scenery for a production or for a particular scene.

naturalism
Representation in performance which is as close as possible to real life.

Aural

- What do want your audience to hear?

  - sound effects
  - live music
  - recorded music?

- What SFX are vital to the plot?
- What would you include to add atmosphere?
- What would you include to suggest location?
- What would you include to create tension?
- What would you include to create surprise?
- What would you include for laughter or comic effect?
- Music and sound can be very emotive: don't underestimate the effect this could have on your audience.

Spatial

- How would you like to see stage space used?
- What would be your ideal space for this production?

Try to make links between the audience and the stage space. Proxemics are very important. Can you give some examples of how you would choose to position your actors at specific moments and say why this matters? Movement and status might be mentioned here.

Take care that this is *your* work and not a review of a production you have seen. (The evaluation of a live production is a different element of Unit 1.) Imagine that no one could design these elements better than you. Explain how you would create these elements. Communicate your ideas clearly. You may find it helpful to use drawings, sketches and diagrams to give full justification for your choices.

WORKED EXAMPLE

A worked example to illustrate visual elements in Berkoff's *Metamorphosis* could be:

Berkoff is very prescriptive in *Metamorphosis*, especially for his set design. I see that he has a clear vision of how he wants the play to look. He describes the focal point of the set as 'a skeletal framework of steel scaffolding'. Through my own exploration of the character Gregor, I see the practical nature of this central sculpture representing Gregor's bedroom. As Berkoff notes himself, this structure suggests a large beetle-type insect sprawling the stage. I think this is very effective and conveys the non-naturalistic style of the play, with scaffolding representing a bedroom. Significantly, it allows the audience to see inside Gregor's room and see him throughout the play, when sometimes the family cannot. Similarly, the nature of the structure allows Gregor to scale the walls in a beetle-like manner, which would otherwise be near impossible with a conventional room set. Berkoff states that the 'stage is clear of all props', which restricts the production to the use of mime. Should I be given licence to alter the set and ignore Berkoff's notes, I would still keep the set prop-free. This is because through performing in class and exploring the play, I feel that it is in sync with the overall style of the play to use mime only. The mime means that no attention is retracted from the subject matter, which is most important, props often being trivial. The only other set instructions Berkoff gives are that there must be three black stools situated equidistant **downstage** from the cage. I would definitely ensure these were stools and not chairs. More specifically, I would use stools that could be swivelled on. For example, this is because I found that in order for the family to shout to Gregor in a stylised way whilst still sitting on the stools, it is most practical that they can quickly and easily swivel to face Gregor, and then back to face the audience.

DSR
Downstage right (stage direction).

Your exploration notes have to be marked by your teacher in the first instance before they are sent away to be moderated. Every centre will have its own procedure for collecting your coursework in and marking it. Your teacher does not have to tell you the marks that he or she has given your work.

Your work must be all your own unaided work, and you will have to sign a document called an authentication sheet to say this. Without your signature on this particular document, your work will be given zero. This is confirmed on page 55 of the specification when it says: 'In accordance with a revision to the current Code of Practice, any candidate who is unable to provide an authentication statement will receive zero credit for the component.'

As Shakespeare said, 'Neither a borrower nor a lender be.' Apply this to your own notes. In other words, do not lend your notes to anyone else nor ask to borrow from anyone else. If someone was to copy your notes and then it came to light that both sets of notes were the same, you would both receive zero! The collective exploration experience ends once you start compiling your coursework, by which time you should have been given ample opportunity to discuss and develop ideas between you that will then form the basis for your notes to reflect your understanding. Writing up your notes should not be an onerous task which you leave until the end of the unit. Your written work should reflect all that you have learnt in practical sessions which have allowed you to explore both plays in a creative, imaginative and sensitive manner. Another aspect of Unit 1 that requires you to be creative, imaginative and sensitive is your written response to a live production seen as part of the course.

THE RESPONSE TO A PRACTITIONER

As theatre has become more creative and imaginative, particularly in the past 150 years, many directors and theatre companies have adopted the style and principles of leading theatre practitioners. These are people who have certain beliefs about the process and the presentation of theatre that give it a unique and recognisable style. Some plays lend themselves to the principles of one particular practitioner or company style. The most frequently used practitioners are Brecht, Stanislavsky and Artaud, but there are other practitioners out there with some centres now referring to theatrical companies who have a particular style such as Théâtre de Complicité, Kneehigh and Forced Entertainment. You may have seen work by these companies or you may recognise from your own work the challenges described below.

The event of live theatre is a rare chance to deliver all these needs. We can have a collective experience, unique to the group of people the fourth wall

In relation to the traditional proscenium arch, the opening of the arch is often referred to as the fourth wall, with the audience looking through it into the life of the characters. Characters can be confined by the fourth wall – they don't look out at the audience – or they can break the fourth wall, step through the arch and look at the audience and, in some plays, address them directly.

assembled in the theatre. I don't want **the fourth wall** constantly and fearfully placed between the actors and their audience, I want the actors to speak to their accomplices, look at them, to respond to them. I want a celebration, a collective gasp of amazement. I want the world to transform in front of the audiences' eyes and demand that they join in with the game. Theatre is nothing without the engagement of the audience's creativity.

(Emma Rice, Artistic Director of Kneehigh Theatre, writing about Kneehigh Theatre Company's artistic aims, 2008; see www.kneehigh.co.uk)

INTERPRETATION

Occasionally, playwrights give such exacting stage directions and a scene is so obvious that there is only one real way to play it. Many directors remove the stage directions from plays before starting rehearsals with their companies so no one approaches the text with any preconceived ideas. However, part of the excitement about producing a play is that the director can interpret things in his or her own way to fit in with his or her overall concept of the play. Shakespeare's plays are wide open to interpretation, not only because there are almost no stage directions but also because of the richness of the language and the subtleties of the text. Only recently, Nicholas Hytner directed Shakespeare's comedy *Much Ado about Nothing* and delighted the critics with his interpretation of Benedick and Beatrice. Instead of the feisty sparring partners that audiences often see, Zoë Wanamaker and Simon Russell Beale make sense of the text in a different way by showing cautious, guarded feelings that alter their expectations of what is to come and, perhaps more importantly from our point of view as drama practitioners, also those of the audience.

WORKED EXAMPLE

A worked example to illustrate the effects of interpreting text in Miller's *A View from the Bridge* is given below. Because it is difficult to separate the play into individual areas, this example also touches on characterisation and language.

Throughout the play, it is possible to interpret how much status a particular character has. Those who remain calm, for instance Alfieri and Beatrice, hold the higher status.

'Eddie I'm a lawyer. I can only deal in what's provable' shows Alfieri maintaining his integrity and status as he refuses to go against his morals. When performing an extract of the play in a small group, we discussed what importance there is over whether you deliver the lines with an accent or not. I felt that as our task was to 'explore' the play, it was not that important. I felt it was more vital to place emphasis on the delivery and tone of the language and to try to interpret Miller's intentions accurately. For example, when playing Eddie and attempting an Italian-American accent, I found much of the crucial emotion needed in delivery was lost, and, owing to too much concentration on the dialect, much of the detail of the character was lost.

VOCABULARY

Your teacher will guide you through the process of developing your vocabulary in relation to the demands of this course and will indicate for you the specific areas of exploration your notes should cover. It would be really good if you could get into the habit of making notes at every opportunity during the course. The very simple reason for this is that you will forget if you do not write down important moments during the exploration of the two Unit 1 texts – it is also good practice for the future. Your teacher may even give you a notebook to record your progress in, but, if not, it will be a good investment for you to buy your own. It is worth mentioning again that the quality of written communication will feature heavily in this specification, and Unit 1 is the starting point. You may not have chosen this subject because you enjoy writing – and you are probably not the only one – but the fact is you have to get used to writing on demand in response to the specific tasks set across the specification.

WORD LIMITS ARE THE LIMIT

Look back to the Golden Rules of getting started (p. 17). Much as you may relish the opportunity to write at great length for this, and any other unit, there is a very strict word limit in place that your teacher will reinforce with you as you go through the first term of the course and that we expand on later in this section.

The 3,000-word maximum is just that – a maximum – and must not be exceeded. Whenever there is a limit in the specification, then that must be adhered to: you can be under but not over the limit. This is why the notebook is so important: you can record your experiences as you go along, and then this information can be distilled into the 3,000 words that you submit for the unit. Hopefully, you will be able to get some practice of recording lesson activity during the induction period so you know the kind of things that may be helpful to you when it comes to preparing your final notes.

10 Evaluation of live theatre

As a drama student, you should want to see as much live theatre as possible. Visiting the theatre is a wonderful thing to do and an important part of our cultural heritage in Britain. We feel sure that there is nowhere else in the world where you can see the wealth and diversity and superb standard of live theatre than in Britain today. There are, of course, good productions abroad, but it is the sheer number of theatres and touring companies that makes it so easy for you to see so much.

Extension Activity

Increase your subject knowledge

If you haven't done so already, it is a good idea to get on the mailing lists of your local theatres. It is easy enough to do this by email. (Be careful which boxes you tick with regards to marketing, although obviously you are asking for certain information to be sent to you.) If you live in a town or city that has a theatre, then just call in and ask to be included on its mailing list. It is the only way of being sure you keep up to date with what's on. Many theatres recognise the importance of attracting younger audiences and will have a range of offers which may include free membership of priority-booking schemes.

If you are visiting London, you can call in to your local tourist-information branch and they will give you free the twice-monthly copy of the *London Theatre Guide* which tells you what is on in London at that time. It also includes the running times of performances, which is essential if you are relying on public transport to get home. If you live in London, the theatre guide is readily available.

GETTING THEATRE TICKETS (CHEAPLY)

Our students often ask us to recommend websites for cheap tickets and up-to-date theatre information. Two sites which are really useful are:

- http://www.whatsonstage.com
- http://www.officiallondontheatre.com.

However, it is probably most useful to build up a directory of theatres you visit in your own favourites section as shown in Figure 10.1.

Figure 10.1
Add theatres to your favourites list.

Another 'favourite' folder below is listed as Drama Schools.

This list could go on and on.
Obviously you will only add those that are most relevant to your location or the places you visit

One of the most useful sites is www.whatsonstage because it has such a good search engine. You can search by date, location, play name or even special offers. This site covers the whole of the UK. The site also includes reviews, and you can even add your own review once you've seen a production. Similarly, the www.officiallondontheatre site is extremely helpful although, as the name suggests, it just covers London.

You are a student and should make the most of this status by getting cheaper tickets (and travel) at every available opportunity. It is always worth asking for student discounts. Lots of theatres have special rates which are not always advertised, especially for people aged from sixteen to twenty-four. Offers at the time of writing for this age range include £5.99 tickets at Birmingham Repertory Theatre, £5 at The Courtyard Theatre in Stratford,

Figure 10.2
Official London Theatre Guide.
The tab marked 'Buy theatre
tickets' is useful for last-minute
cheap seats.

and the National Theatre in London regularly have £10 Travelex tickets. Lots of offers come and go, but it is always worth asking: it can be as easy as taking proof of identity and age with you when collecting tickets from the box office. An NUS (National Union of Students) card is ideal for this, but so is a driving licence or a proof-of-age card. The advantage of the NUS card is that it entitles you to other discounts. In the Sixth Form, you are able to apply for the NUS associate card (http://www.nusonline.co.uk/associate).

The Half-Price Ticket Booth in London now has a permanent building in Leicester Square. Not all the London theatres use the Half-Price Ticket Booth to sell their available seats, but it is a most useful service. Its website contains an important warning about not buying from ticket touts or unknown sources, and we would certainly support this.

Of course, one of the most obvious places to buy theatre tickets is directly from the theatre itself. The advantage of buying them in person at the theatre box office is that you can see the seating plan and you don't have to pay a booking fee. The addition of a booking fee is a controversial issue, and especially when you are on a limited budget, the booking fee can come as a nasty shock. Always try to deal with the theatre directly, always ask for a student discount, and, if you are going with a group of friends, always ask if there is a group rate.

Do not rely solely on your school or college to take you to the theatre. If you are capable of going into town on your own, you are capable of going to the theatre!

Some theatre box offices will redirect your telephone call to one of the larger booking agencies, usually Ticketmaster or Seetickets. They do charge a booking fee, although may offer discounts with a valid NUS card.

Figure 10.3
The Half-Price Ticket Booth.

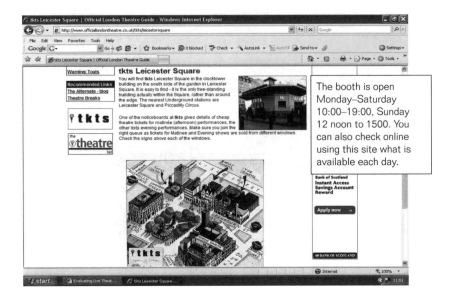

Almost every theatre in the country accepts theatre tokens. These make a great present to either give or receive and are worth putting on birthday or Christmas lists if friends or family want to buy you something that they consider 'educational'.

FIRST NIGHTS AND PUBLIC DRESS REHEARSALS

dress rehearsal
Usually the rehearsal just before the first performance when everybody must wear full costume. The dress rehearsal is as close as possible to the actual performance without an audience present (usually!). It is often combined with a technical rehearsal where any effects and lighting or sound cues are tested and perfected to see that they work under performance conditions.

Some theatres offer incredible deals for public **dress rehearsals**. They can even be free or often just a nominal charge such as £1. An example of this would be Sheffield Crucible Theatre which often has public dress rehearsals that cost only £1.

Extension Activity

Two performances of a production

If a production is of particular interest to you, it can be a fascinating exercise to see it twice during its 'run'. You will almost certainly see how the production has developed and evolved. You could do this by seeing it at the public dress rehearsal and then again a few weeks later nearer the end of its run.

Figure 10.4
The Gate Theatre, Dublin.
Source: Liam White/Alamy.

POST-SHOW DISCUSSIONS, TALKBACKS, MEET THE COMPANY

Many productions have extra sessions before or after the show when you can learn more about certain aspects of the production. These are either free or cost relatively little. They are usually advertised, but again it's worth asking when you book your tickets. If you are a design student, it may be worth

Figure 10.5
Kneehigh Theatre Company in rehearsal.
Source: © Steve Tanner.

booking a backstage tour, as that way you may get to see the set of the production you are going to watch. It can be most illuminating to actually stand on the set of a production that you then watch from the **auditorium**, where things will look quite different. Some companies offer workshops working with the actors on the set.

auditorium
Where the audience sits. In traditional theatres, the audience and performers are separated by a curtain.

VOLUNTEER OR ASK FOR WORK EXPERIENCE

As an industry, arts organisations in Britain have an enormous impact on the economy and, of course, employ large numbers of people. You could always look for a part-time job in a theatre, which may in turn entitle you to free theatre tickets. Many regional theatres could not run without the generous help of volunteers who often sell programmes or do other jobs. Volunteering always looks good on your CV or personal statement and would definitely lend weight to applications for drama-related courses.

Work experience in theatres is very popular, and there are always more people wanting places than there are spaces. Some of you will have already found this out if you were looking for placements in Year 10 or 11. However, many theatres are more keen to take slightly older students, particularly if you are prepared to go during holiday times or in the evenings. The key is to apply early. Some theatres hold auditions or interviews even for work placements, and, with increased health and safety regulations, structured week-long placements are becoming more common.

Figure 10.6
Everyman Theatre, Liverpool.

Source: © Andrew Jankunas/ Alamy.

BECOME A THEATRE CRITIC

You can do this officially, by approaching your local newspaper and asking if they are interested in a young person's view on local shows. Your school or college may have a newspaper, newsletter or magazine. It is quite possible that if you offered your services as a regular reviewer, you should be able to negotiate 'free' tickets with your local theatre. Even if you don't review theatre productions for another party, it is an excellent idea to start your own notebook *now* and record your thoughts and opinions on each and every play you see. An easy option to this is to keep a ticket album of all the productions you see. Drama schools and drama courses at university almost always ask you about productions you have seen, so it will be useful and impressive if you can produce your ticket or review notebook.

What's the difference between evaluating live theatre and a theatre review? Some people are paid to write reviews of theatre productions. Michael Billington is one of the leading theatre critics in Britain today. He joined the *Guardian* newspaper in 1971 and has written reviews of plays ever since. He admits that sometimes he gets things wrong, but even after thirty-plus years in the same job, he is enthusiastic about what he does: 'People ask me how I keep going and retain my apparent enthusiasm. The short, Johnsonian answer is that the man or woman who is bored with theatre is bored with life' (http://blogs.guardian.co.uk/authors/michael_billington/ profile.html).

Figure 10.7
Keep a record of the plays you have seen by keeping your tickets.

Extension Activity

Published reviews

- Choose a play that you have seen recently and find three different reviews that were written about it. How far do you agree with the reviews?
- An average newspaper review is about 500 words long. Write your own review of the production in just 500 words.

Everyone is entitled to their opinion about whether they like a particular production or not. The important thing is to know *why* you do or don't like it. We mentioned earlier that you can add your own review to the Whatsonstage.co.uk website, and, in today's technological society, there are many theatre blogs and instant-opinion sites all over the Internet. Michael Billington's reaction to this modern phenomenon is to say:

Although in principle, I'm all for blogs, I still cherish the idea of the printed review. The restrictions of space and time are considerable, but they force one to focus on essentials. A blog is more like an informal letter: a review, if it's to have any impact, has to have a definable structure. The critic, unlike the blogger, also has a duty to set any play or performance in its historical context.

(www.guardian.co.uk, 17 September 2007)

There is much good advice here to you as a drama student because you also have a restriction on space (in this case, 1,000 words) and, yet, your evaluation needs impact, structure and an awareness of historical context.

The ability to write in a concise manner observing a prescribed word limit is an invaluable skill that makes for focused learning and a good use of time. Students will find that this will stand them in good stead for Unit 4 of the specification.

PREPARING TO WRITE YOUR EVALUATION OF LIVE THEATRE

Possibly the most important thing to bear in mind is that you are *not* evaluating the *play,* you are evaluating the *performance.* You need to be very clear that you understand the difference between these two things. I could say, 'I don't like the play *Mother Courage,* but I did like this particular production of it.' Or, conversely, 'I really like the play *Mother Courage,* but I didn't like this particular production of it.' It is very easy to confuse the two, but if you remember that this is a Drama and Theatre Studies course and not English Literature, it will help you focus on the fact that the production and how it is performed is what really concerns us.

ALL THEATRE IS GOOD THEATRE: TRUE OR FALSE?

You could debate this question for years to come because the fact is that until *you* see a particular production, you cannot know if it is good or bad. Your drama teacher will be able to advise you on whether or not a production is likely to be good, often based on evidence such as whether the theatre has a good reputation, the company is well known and the actors are well known, but, in truth, so many different factors contribute to making a whole production that there are no guarantees. Several years ago, a group of AS students saw a touring production from quite a well-known theatre company. They hated the production, finding it laughable. The actors were 'wooden', the music was badly recorded, the songs were dubbed (it was a production of a play by Brecht) and the set was inappropriate and distracting. However, this experience was not wasted as it gave them a benchmark with which to judge other productions they saw and also served as a useful guide when doing their own performance work. Obviously, it would be disheartening to see too many productions that you felt were poor, but the important thing is to learn from these experiences. Another example involves a more recent visit to the National Theatre in London dividing both critics and students with Katie Mitchell's production of Don Taylor's version of *The Women of Troy*. The production really seemed to polarise opinion, but the most important aspect of it from a student of drama's point of view was that it did provoke such diverse reactions and enabled a real debate to take place about the theatrical experience. This production was presented at the National Theatre, with the implication therefore being that it represented the best that the country had to offer, and expectations were understandably high. From your point of view, of course, the issues of 'good or bad' and 'I liked it or I disliked it' do not need to effect your evaluation. They may well inform it, but the criteria are based on the quality of your written evaluation and how far you are able to demonstrate your understanding of the experience on the page.

The assessment criteria for a top-band evaluation says: 'Student's evaluation of a live theatre performance is outstanding. They are fully aware of a wide range of production values and are able to analyse the effect this may have on an audience. Supported examples are detailed and reported with almost faultless accuracy.' You cannot expect to produce an outstanding evaluation on the first piece of theatre you see. You have approximately two terms to see at least *one* live performance, but if you went to the theatre once a month between September and Easter of your AS year, you would gain valuable experience and knowledge while seeing approximately six productions. The production you choose to evaluate may be a production you see of one of the two plays you study and write about in your exploration notes or it may be a different play. Be advised by your teacher. Many students do well when they see a good range of live theatre on organised trips or independently but submit their evaluation on a play that has been 'taught' by their teacher. The advantage of evaluating a production that you have all seen as a drama group is that you can discuss it together, and your teacher may encourage you to explore elements within it that you hadn't previously considered.

Extension Activity

Write a practice evaluation

Early on in the course, you could see a production on your own and write an evaluation of it quite independently of your drama teacher, then ask them to mark it. This would give you an early indication of how you were doing and areas to focus on next time you saw a production. Your teacher-examiner will have a set of criteria against which your evaluation will be assessed. It would be good to have a copy of that early in the course. In some schools and colleges, all the assessment criteria are blown up, laminated and displayed in the drama studio so everybody is aware of where they are going.

WHAT SHOULD YOU PUT IN AN EVALUATION?

Production values

We often talk about 'production values' which basically means:

- Was the performance theatrical?
- Did they make good use of the resources available to them?
- Was there a sense of occasion?

Production values are all the elements that come together to make a vibrant production that has strong theatrical qualities. They can be a combination of any or all of the following:

- lighting
- acting
- sound
- **FX**
- proxemics
- costume
- audience
- make-up
- live music
- masks
- special FX
- puppets
- voice props

FX effects
Usually sound effects in the theatre.

- **physicality** of the actors
- set
- body
- language
- staging
- interpretation

physicality
An actor's ability to embody a character by use of movement and gesture.

Performance not play

There is always the temptation to write about the *play,* and we have seen many students do this when in actual fact, the marks are awarded for an evaluation of the *production* seen. Consider the following example, which illustrates the point we are making in a few lines: '*Measure for Measure* is often referred to as "problem" play as it does not fit any of the conventional Shakespearian categories, such as comedy, tragedy, etc. It is about the abuse of power and how justice eventually . . .'

Do not do this! The student has written thirty-five words describing the *play,* which is not what this task asks for. You must assume that the play is known well to both your drama teacher and the moderator who may eventually be reading your evaluation. If you find that you just can't help yourself from writing about the play, then do so in order to get it out of the way but do not submit this work for marking: see it as a preliminary exercise to allow you to focus on the main task. You may not know the play well before you see it in performance and may read it, whether extracts, or in its entirety, after you have seen it. Your evaluation in Unit 1 may be on a performance of one of the two texts you are exploring, but it does not have to be.

HOW TO START

NAME OF PLAY   by NAME OF PLAYRIGHT

Performed by NAME OF COMPANY

At: NAME OF THEATRE   on: DATE SEEN

Figure 10.8
Keeping a notebook, I.

Figure 10.9
Keeping a notebook, II.

This could be:

Henry V by William Shakespeare
Performed by The Royal Shakespeare Company
At: the Courtyard Theatre, Stratford-On-Avon   on: 5 January 2009

ON THE DAY

As soon as you enter the auditorium, you should be able to pick up clues about the play you are going to watch. For this reason alone, take your seat as soon as the house doors open. In a traditional **proscenium-arch** theatre, the curtains may be closed at this point although this is increasingly unusual in the theatre today. In traditional theatres, the director and designer often choose to strip the stage bare so that the set is already visible to the audience as they enter. This is called the **pre-set**.

proscenium arch
The actual opening of the frame itself, which often forms the boundary between performers and audience, particularly in more traditional theatre with performers not stepping outside it during the performance.

pre-set
The stage space as set before the production starts and what the audience sees when the curtains open or the lights go up.

Look around you

- What can you see?
- What is suggested by the staging, if anything?
- How is it lit?
- Is there any music playing?
- Who else is there?
- Does it look as though you are typical members of this audience?

In these few minutes before the performance actually begins, this can be a useful moment to sketch the set, you can always add to it at the interval.

Do not write notes during a performance, it is very rude to the actors, and you will miss many things about the performance itself. It is also distracting for other members of the audience who may not be drama students. Clearly, you must be alert to what is happening during the performance, and you must record as much as you can remember, but you are part of a group, and, between you, there will be a collective memory of the event. See yourself as an active participant in the performance, rather than a passive observer.

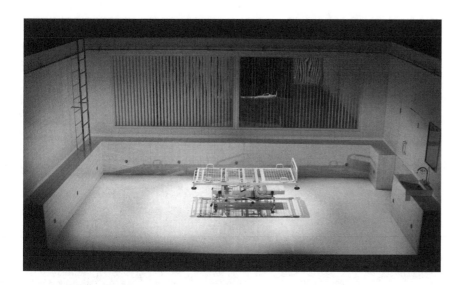

Figure 10.10
Set design for *Pool (No Water)*, Frantic Assembly.

Source: © Scott Graham.

Your evaluation could begin with your first impressions of what you saw and heard on the stage. What would be your first impressions here? Look at the following examples of first impressions of various productions:

- 'We could see the interior of a 1920s drawing room; this immediately created the effect of . . .'
- 'The stage was bare apart from a very contemporary coffee table and an animal print rug. Amy Winehouse music was playing very loudly, and the effect was exciting, I felt as if we were about to glimpse the inside of someone's life. However, as soon as the play started, the atmosphere changed . . .'
- 'The Director had decided to have some of the actors already on the set as the audience entered the auditorium. They were all going about their business in the factory, concentrating on their work. It created a quiet mood in the audience as they watched this while taking their seats. The moment the owner of the factory entered, the actors stood to attention, and the play began. His costume obviously singled him out as he looked different to the workers: the fabrics were more expensive, and the jacket, cravat, top hat and cane indicated his status. Before he even spoke, his body language was authoritative: he walked briskly with a straight back and a stern expression.'

Something will always happen to signify that the play has started.

- Do the house lights dim?
- Do the stage lights come up?

Figure 10.11

Natalya Tena as Fevvers in *Nights at the Circus*, Kneehigh Theatre Company.

Source: © Steve Tanner.

- Is there music?
- Is there a sound effect or other audible clue?

Occasionally, there are actors already on the set when the audience enters the auditorium. This is a technique often used by companies such as Kneehigh, who will sometimes also have the actors in role but mingling with the audience, maybe singing or playing music. They have even been known to place actors in the auditorium. In their production of *Nights at the Circus*, one of the actors was sitting in the middle of the stalls, and about five minutes into the play he stood up and shouted out to the actors on the stage. This gave the audience quite a shock until they realised he was part of the company. This technique is called placing a 'plant'. In other words, the actor was already planted (or placed) there before the show began.

In the Kneehigh production of *Brief Encounter*, two seats were reserved on the front row and were occupied by two of the actors several times during the performance when they appeared to be watching something on the stage.

DURING THE PERFORMANCE

During the actual performance, there are many questions you can be asking. Use the prompt sheet provided opposite to make rough notes before expanding them into your formal response. In the vast majority of cases, your teacher will lead you in a discussion session on the production in order for you to collect your thoughts and have enough information to enable you to complete your evaluation.

NOTES TO CONSIDER WHILE EVALUATING LIVE THEATRE

Technical details

- Describe the following and how they were used:

  - lighting (LFX);
  - sound (SFX);
  - set;
  - special effects.

- What type of stage is being used? Is it a 'traditional' proscenium arch, a **thrust stage**, **traverse**, theatre-in-the-round or something completely different such as **promenade** theatre?

What did you see? (visual aspects)

- Props
- Costume
- Settings
- Anything else?

Acting

- How did the actors portray characters? (Use the actors' names, not their character names.)
- How did they use language? Select two or three highlights from the production as a whole to illustrate your opinions.

Audience

- Was there any audience involvement/participation?
- Did the audience seem to like the performances? How do you know?
- Did you like the performances? How do you know?

thrust stage
A stage that comes out into the audience that creates a platform for the actors very close to the audience. Traditionally this is associated with the Globe Theatre.

traverse
A performance space in which the audience sit in rows facing each other with the action taking place down the centre of the space between them.

promenade
A style of theatre in which the audience moves amongst the action that takes place within a defined space with minimal props and that looks back at the medieval performances in town centres and through city streets. Promenade demands real commitment from the audience and control from the actors in order to direct the audience's attention towards where the next scene is going to take place.

Directing/design

- What do you think the Director was trying to achieve/say to the audience?
- Did the play communicate successfully?
- What is your opinion/view of the play in this production of it?
- Did you like the production? Why?

On the page

When you are typing up your evaluation, remember to start your word count and keep a regular check as you go along. You can only use 12-point font, and it is much more practical to use a plain font that is clear to read. Times New Roman, Arial or something similar always work best. Avoid fancy, flowery fonts which are difficult to read.

Extension Activity

Types of stages

Find out about the various types of staging mentioned above. Keep notes, and simple diagrams, in your drama notebook for future reference.

EVALUATING NOT REPORTING

The overall task is an evaluation of a play you have seen in performance. Remember that general statements will *not* gain high marks. For example, the following sort of sentences are much too general – and simplistic:

- I thought the acting was good.
- The costumes were effective.
- I liked the set and the way it was lit.
- Richard Griffiths played a good part.
- The whole audience was in tears at the end.
- I laughed at the funny bits.
- Some of it was dull but not all of it.

All of these statements might have elements of truth in them, and they may be the kind of throwaway remarks you might make to friends as you are leaving the theatre, but, as students of drama you need to be able to expand on all of these statements to create clear examples to support your understanding of the experience you have had and to communicate that to others.

You have to start somewhere – and your GCSE Drama experience may be a useful reminder here as you think about how to structure evaluation.

KEY WORDS

In evaluating live performances, you may need to think about the following key words:

- because
- for example
- for instance

A more constructive example of an evaluation would be:

WORKED EXAMPLE

Lucy Waring was particularly convincing as Nora when she lied to her husband. She showed this physically, for example, by staring straight ahead into the audience and looked as if she had no connection to her comfortable sitting room and her acceptable married life. She conveyed her nervous anxiety to the audience by laughing loudly, almost hysterically, then jumping when her husband finally spoke to her.

Extension Activity

Background to the playwright

It is usually possible to find out about the life of the playwright. Is there any aspect of their life that may have any bearing on the play and the performance of it? (Be careful: there may not be anything obvious here, and your evaluation is about the performance not the play nor, indeed, the life of the playwright!)

Remember the word count rules . . . For Unit 1, you must keep your evaluation of your live theatre experience under 1,000 words. Your work will not be marked beyond this point, and, as a long-term exercise, it is good practice to stick to limits and guidelines as well as deadlines. The evaluation of *Tristan and Yseult* by a Year 12 student that follows is 932 words long and will give you some idea of what length you are aiming for.

WORKED EXAMPLE

Tristan and Yseult

On Thursday 17 November, we went to the Birmingham Rep to see Kneehigh's production *Tristan and Yseult*. I thoroughly enjoyed the performance, for numerous reasons.

The most striking thing about Kneehigh is their originality. Their approach to theatre is bold and energetic. We heard the company give a talk before the performance, which was very useful in helping me understand the reasons and explanations behind the theatre we were about to see. I also volunteered to join them on the stage for a demonstration, and they showed us how specifically they worked as a team. During a short space of time they were able to incorporate two of us into what appeared to be an intricate fight scene, but with the help of everyone else in the **cast** it worked seamlessly.

One of the company's founding members, Mike Shepard (Managing Director), told us that one of their mottos was 'Fear Is Useless', and I thought this was portrayed wonderfully thorough their production.

When the performance began, I immediately noticed that although it was in no way a pantomime, they still made the audience feel involved. This made sense as they had told us previously that their work was originally exclusively outdoors, where it was near impossible to ignore your audience due to the light on them and the close proximity between them and the actors.

Their use of space on the stage was superb. The band was integrated into the action, and, at all times, the majority of the cast was on stage in some way. Not only was the set intricate and large, but it also created different dimensions on the stage for the play to work around. For example, the stairway linked the central disc (which was the main focus of the stage) with the upper scaffolding: not only did this provide access to a higher focus point, but it also drew the attention further **upstage**. However, the most impressive feature of the set was the

---

cast

As a verb to assign roles to the actors. The cast is the list of characters in the play and the names of the actors playing them.

upstage

The area towards the back of the acting area, away from the audience. Called upstage because of its association with raked theatre and the fact that this part of the stage would be higher than the downstage area, that closest to the audience.

central discs and subsequent pole. This was used to great effect in many different ways. Sections of the disc could be lifted out to create extra levels. The central pole provided ropes to support both actors and to lift out sections of the disc. This was used most notably during the 'Intoxication Dance' between Tristan and Yseult, climaxing in a spectacular kiss. As Tristan Sturrock (Tristan) and Éva Magyar (Yseult) were flying around the set on these ropes, they needed to be supported by other members of the company who were used as a counterbalance. This was crucial in the smooth running and safety of the actors, and therefore demonstrated the trust within the company.

Figure 10.12
The actors fly around the set on ropes, Kneehigh Theatre Company.

Source: © Steve Tanner.

One of the things I enjoyed the most about the performance was the storytelling element. They cleverly used the 'Love-Spotters' as both a means of telling the story, helping it flow and keeping the actors on stage under the guise of an anorak and a balaclava. It was as if you were carried along the story with them, and their quick and energetic approach meant they would not allow you to lose interest in the piece. They used many different ways to deliver the story, such as narration, choral speaking and song. It is impossible to say who the star performers were, because they were all as one. They believed this was mostly due to the way in which they prepare and rehearse for a production. They work in some small barns in Cornwall where they have complete artistic freedom, where, in their words, 'there are no rules'. This helps them develop a feeling of unity, which allows them to truly bond as a company. In turn, they become a real ensemble when on stage. As I have said, this is then directly conveyed through their work; and I love it!

Technically, their performance was extremely accurate and sharp. Because they have such a physical and energetic style on stage, you realise that the technical aspects of the drama are worked out to a much finer degree than is first apparent. They incorporated the use of live music using their own band on stage. At times, the actors too were involved with the music, and vice versa. Despite common safety precautions, they used real flames at the end of the play to give greater depth and emotion to the final scene. This was a highly effective method that created both romance and tragedy.

Occasionally, they used **melodrama** to emphasise moments in the story, and this was very effective. One example was when there needed to be a switch between Yseult and her maid – a device used in theatre throughout time. This was made even funnier, because the maid was in fact a man! But even this was forgotten very easily as you were carried along with the magic of the play.

In conclusion, I can find little or no fault with this production. I was spellbound from the start. At the interval, I found myself unable to get up to buy an ice cream due to my fits of laughter and, yet, at the end, I

melodrama

A style of performance developed in the latter half of the nineteenth century which had a major influence on the early days of British cinema. Melodramas were known for their 'stock' characters of villain, heroine and hero, and they were often based on real-life characters – William Corder and his murder victim, Maria Marten, for example.

Figure 10.13

The actors in disguise, Kneehigh Theatre Company.

Source: © Steve Tanner.

found a lump in my throat. When Kneehigh tell you a story, you are not only told it, but you empathise with the situations. (This is clearly a house style, because subsequently I went to see their next production, *Nights at the Circus*.) They filled an extremely large space with vibrant energy and bold physicality; the music was fantastic; the acting exciting and their unity remarkable. I only wish I was able to catch it again at the end of its tour!

(With thanks to Jake Waring, a Year 12 Drama and Theatre Studies student) Bibliography

PLAYS MENTIONED IN PART II

Ayckbourn, Alan (1974) *Absurd Person Singular*, London: Samuel French.
Berkoff, Steven (1969) *Metamorphosis*, London: Amber Lane Press.
Brecht, Bertolt (1943) *The Life of Galileo*, London: Methuen.
—— (2007) *The Caucasian Chalk Circle*, London: Penguin
Euripides (1992) *The Trojan Women*, London: Penguin.
Ibsen, Henrik (1996) *A Doll's House*, London: Faber and Faber.
Miller, Arthur (1947) *All My Sons*, London: Methuen.
—— (1995) *A View from the Bridge*, London: Methuen.
—— (1953) *The Crucible*, London: Methuen.
Priestley, J. B. (1947) *An Inspector Calls*, London: Penguin.
Shakespeare, William (1623) *Measure for Measure*.
—— (1597) *Romeo and Juliet*.
—— (1603) *Hamlet*.

OTHER USEFUL READING

Bial Henry and Martin Carol (eds) (1999) *Brecht Sourcebook*, London and New York: Routledge.
McEvoy, Sean (2006) *Shakespeare: The Basics*, London: Routledge.
Miller, Arthur (1987) *Timebends*, Harmondsworth: Penguin.
Shapiro, James (2006) *1599*, London: Faber.
Willett, John (trans.) (1964) *Brecht on Theatre*, London: Methuen.
Wood, Michael (2003) *Shakespeare*, London: BBC Worldwide.

UNIT 2
THEATRE TEXT IN
PERFORMANCE

PART III

11 Overview of Unit 2

This is your opportunity to demonstrate skills in a performance environment, drawing on your previous experience in exploring the two plays in Unit 1. Your aim in this unit is to deliver a performance to an audience, including your examiner for this unit.

ASSESSMENT OBJECTIVES FOR UNIT 2

- **AO1** (15 per cent): Demonstrate the application of performance and/or production skills through the realisation of drama and theatre.
- **AO3** (15 per cent): Interpret plays from different periods and genres.

There are two sections in this unit. In each section, you can choose to take the role of either a performer or a theatre designer.

In Unit 1, your teacher is your examiner and assesses your contribution to exploration against an agreed national standard of work for the unit. In Unit 2, the examiner is appointed by the Examination Board and will visit your centre on an agreed date to assess your work in relation to the agreed national standard for performance.

The knowledge and understanding you gained during the exploration of the two plays in Unit 1 can now be applied with a view to delivering a performance to an audience. You may also have seen at least one performance as part of the course so far, and there will have been areas of that performance that will have had an impact on you and may give you ideas as you look now at Unit 2. The two AS units merge effectively together, and it may be that your teacher will structure your course to split Unit 1 on either side of Unit 2 to give you an opportunity to perform earlier in the course. This is acceptable and may suit you and your group better than leaving the performance until later in the year.

The performance material you and your teacher choose must be taken from a complete and substantial published play text, essentially something that has an ISBN number. The word 'substantial' is the key here, and your teacher will guide you towards a text of sufficient substance to enable you to be able to access the marks for this unit.

You can choose to be a performer in both sections or a designer in both sections. You can also mix and match and design for one section and perform in the other. Section A is worth the same amount of marks as Section B so deserves your full attention but probably with less direct influence and input from your teacher. Essentially, Section A is about you and your ownership of preparing your chosen skill for examination in relation to the text but this should always be under the guidance – not necessarily direction – of your teacher who is there to support you.

The unit looks like this:

SECTION A

Performer

- Solo (monologue)
- Pair Performance (duologue)

Theatre designer

In support of the performer(s), you should select one of the following:

- costume design
- lighting design
- mask design
- make-up design
- set and props design
- sound design

SECTION B

- Performer within a performance company led by your teacher.
- Theatre designer within a performance company led by your teacher, choosing one or more of the aspects listed above.

A visiting examiner will assess your contribution to both sections, and your work should be presented to an appropriate audience.

AN APPROPRIATE AUDIENCE

An appropriate audience is one that your teacher thinks will respond to the material presented to them. Your performance may be aimed at a particular section of society – for example, younger children, GCSE students, adults – in which case your communication within the chosen performance piece to that particular audience will be assessed by your examiner. A performance of *Grimm Tales* for six-year-old children will be a different performance than the same text aimed at an adult audience, and your examiner will look at this in relation to your contribution within your director's concept or Section B.

Most Unit 2 group performances are aimed at a 'general adult audience, made up of family, friends and teachers', and, therefore, your performance becomes appropriate for a 'general adult audience'.

Your teacher will guide you further on this, but it is not essential to have a wide audience for Section A as long as there are enough people there to make the chosen skill work for you. It may be that Section A is performed to other members of your class or to a group of students from another year group: it does not have to be performed under full performance conditions.

Here is another example from the e-specification available online at www.edexcel.org.uk. You might wish to look up all the assessment criteria yourself as you progress through the course. Your teacher will have access to this information and any updates as they occur, but this particular screen shot summarises Unit 2 for you.

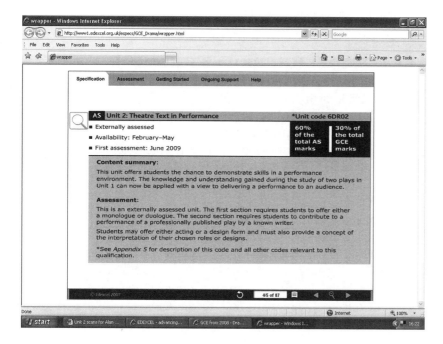

Figure 11.1
The e-specification for Unit 2.

The whole unit is worth 30 per cent of your A-Level marks, and the visiting examiner will be looking for you to meet a number of criteria in order to enable you to access the marks. Your teacher will guide and direct you in order for you to be able to carry out the tasks that follow.

This unit covers a lot of ground, but what it also effectively does is to build on the experience of Unit 1, and you should always have in your mind the skills you are developing to help your understanding of how drama works across the whole of this specification, not just for now but also thinking ahead to the requirements of the A2 year.

PERFORMANCE SKILLS IN UNIT 2

You will learn how to:

* read and research two play texts;
* prepare for two performances;
* work alone or with one other student as a performer for Section A;
* work collaboratively as a member of a performance company for Section B;
* attend rehearsals;
* respond to and work with a director – normally your tutor/teacher;
* understand the interpretation of the theatre text in performance;
* demonstrate an understanding of style and genre;
* communicate the text to an audience.

THEATRE DESIGN SKILLS IN UNIT 2

You will learn how to:

* read and research two play texts;
* prepare chosen skills to support two performances;
* work alone or with one other design student for Section A;
* work collaboratively as a member of a performance company for Section B;
* design and operate you chosen skill in performance;
* respond to and work collaboratively with a director;
* understand how your chosen skill supports the interpretation of the text;
* provide documentation to clarify your preparation work;
* communicate the design skill to an audience in a performance context.

Working closely with your teacher in order to access Unit 2, you need to be aware of the general requirements that follow. See the website or later sections for how your contribution to the performance will be assessed.

THE WRITTEN CONCEPT

For Section A, both performing and design candidates compile a written performance or design concept for the response to the chosen text. If you are a performer, then you need only to complete a written concept for Section A. If you are a designer, then you need to complete a written concept for the section(s) that you are designing for.

The written concept must be no longer than 500 words. This must be sent to the visiting examiner at least seven working days before the date of the examination. Your written concept will typically arise out of a preparation period during which you make notes, experiment and reach performance or design conclusions which are then detailed in your concept. Your examiner will give a mark out of ten for your concept which is, effectively, to demonstrate your understanding and to give a statement of intent for your examiner.

DECISIONS YOU NEED TO MAKE

Unit 2 is really about *performance,* and this is *your* opportunity to engage in an aspect of performance which you then share with a visiting examiner. It all seems very straightforward, but there are decisions that you have to make in order for you to be able to access the marks for this unit and to reach your full potential. Clearly, your teacher will guide you and support you through the Unit 2 process, and there are connections you can make with the experience of Unit 1. Your teacher is your director for Unit 2, Section B and will guide you in your preparation for Section A. The decisions you make are:

- Section A:

  - Design or perform?
  - Monologue or duologue?

- Section B:

  - Design or perform?

The vast majority of students will offer performance for this Unit. This does not mean that you have to, of course, but it does mean that you need to think very carefully about what is required for each element. Your visiting examiner, against a set of published criteria, assesses both skills, and there is absolutely no difference in the response of your examiner to whichever skill you choose. You have equal access to the marks whether you are a theatre designer or a performer – or a mixture of both – for this unit.

Before you decide, you might like to consider the options carefully, and your teacher will have a professional judgement to offer on this as well, as to some extent will other members of your group.

Theatre design is not an easy option, but if you enjoy this creative aspect of performance it can be very rewarding and challenging. You need to ask yourself and your teacher some very simple questions right at the start of the Unit 2 process in order for you to be able to reach the right decision about the theatre-design option:

- What might I offer in relation to costume, lighting, mask, make-up, set, props or sound in relation to my director's interpretation of the play for Section B?
- What do I need to do and produce in order to be able to meet the minimum evidence requirements as a theatre-design candidate in Section A and/or Section B?
- What will my relationship be with the rest of my performance group and the director in Section B, and how will I be able to fit in with choices people make in Section A?
- What do I do during rehearsals?
- What do I have to do on the day of the exam performance – what is the visiting examiner looking for and what evidence will I need?
- Will I have to do it all myself, or will there be support from the rest of the group and the director?

The Examiner says:

The decision to offer theatre design for this unit has to be a positive one and will suit those students who have a particular creative ability in relation to at least one of the specified elements. There will be a learning opportunity in creating your design element in relation to the Section B group performance and in being part of the performance group, all of who will have a major impact on the look and feel of the final performance. Your creative input in Section A is a challenge, and it is probably advisable that you work in conjunction with a performance student to support a monologue or, preferably, a duologue offered for examination. It can appear quite daunting at first but you should be just as supported in the process as the performance candidates will be.

You can choose to offer a theatre-design skill for both sections. This is perfectly acceptable as it is a clear option choice within the specification, and an examiner assessing your work will assess it against the criteria, not against your other design contribution. You do not need to feel that you should be offering a design skill in Section A and an acting skill in Section B just because you think the examiner will expect this: the examiner will assess you against the criteria, whatever the skill or combination of skills you offer.

Whatever your decisions, it is really important that you talk things through with your teacher to ensure that the facilities you have in your school or college will support your decisions. It can be a daunting prospect stepping out too far from the group, but that does not mean you should not do it.

There may be more to the design option than first appears so please check it out carefully as the 60 per cent of the marks for your AS year that the examiner has to award will need to be earned in the same way as the performance candidates earn their 60 per cent (30 per cent of the total A-Level course).

Remember, if you choose to offer design for Section B, you will be working closely with the teacher-director, creating your chosen design concept alongside his or her interpretation of the play, in exactly the same way as the performers within the piece will respond to direction. You need to know and understand the text, but, more importantly, you need to present a concept that reflects an understanding of the style, genre and overall demands of the production. You need to be aware of the demands in terms of assessment evidence to be presented to your examiner, not least of which is your presentation of your ideas, which needs to last up to ten minutes. This should be rehearsed in exactly the same way as the performing candidates will rehearse their role or roles for the piece. It would be unwise to stand up on the day, not having rehearsed your presentation in front of others, preferably your group and your teacher.

Look carefully at what is demanded of you as a designer in both sections before making the final decision. Consider the options and go for it – if it is for you.

DECISION MADE: PERFORMER

Now that you are a performer, you must decide whether you are to perform on your own or with another member of your group. Have a look around you at your fellow students and think back to work you have been involved in so far. It may be that your immediate reaction is to go for the duologue as there is safety in numbers, if nothing else, but you need to consider all the possibilities of both options before deciding. Half of your marks for this unit depend on this decision, and it cannot be made lightly: it has to be considered carefully and with your best interests in mind. It is no good being bounced into making a decision that you then regret just because you feel sorry for somebody who might be left out or you are worried about being left out yourself. What do *you* want to do?

Extension Activity

Thinking time break

OK, too many questions, too many decisions to be made, and you have no idea what you really want to do here. Take five minutes to get your thoughts together in the following way:

- Grab a sheet of paper or fold a page in half in your notebook.
- On one half write 'for' on the other 'against'.
- Under each heading list as many reasons for or against monologue as you can think of in five minutes.
- If that does not do it for you, start again and write as many reasons for or against duologue you can think of and then compare the lists.

If you are still stumped after this, then you may really, deep down inside, be thinking you ought to be looking at the design option.

All right, now that you have decided, how do you make it happen? Look at the assessment descriptors. The examiner will focus on these as you perform and award marks only in the categories listed. If you are *not* working with a theatre-design candidate for your monologue or duologue, for example, there are no marks for creating an elaborate costume, set or lighting plot for yourself. The examiner is looking at your performance of the chosen piece – nothing else. A piece of costume or a vital prop and a neutral lighting state will probably be enough for you to indicate your role and to support your monologue or duologue. There really is no need for anything else.

Section A

In Section A, you must choose a suitable play text from which you will select your performance piece. It is essential that you consider the entire play text so that you are aware of where and how your performance piece fits the whole play, and you are able to write your rationale based on this information.

Section B

If you are offering performance skills in Section B, you will be working under the direction of your teacher on the group piece. The criteria are similar to those for Section A and the decision to perform in the group piece is probably a straightforward one for you to make.

DECISION MADE: DESIGNER

There are students every year who take this course because they are keen on the technical aspects of theatre. If this is you, then this unit could be the highlight of your AS year. You need to make the decision carefully though, really consider the information we present for you here and listen to your teacher who has the complete overview of the course and an understanding of the kind of things that the examiner is looking for on the day. It could be a very lonely existence being the only design candidate if you are not careful and if you do not have a supportive group around you and a teacher who is prepared to guide you and the others towards your achievement.

It is a fact that some teachers will not encourage the design option for a variety of reasons, the most important one of which is the lack of facilities to enable you to access the marks. In some cases, teachers do not feel confident in guiding you, and this also needs to be taken into account.

The class may influence your decision too: it can be a difficult task being a designer for a duologue in which the two performers are building up a relationship from which you are largely excluded. Design for Section B will mean that you are closely working with your teacher as director, and you need to consider the implications of this too as your design will be assessed alongside the overall performance concept. There is a lot to consider and a lot of decisions you will have to make on your own or as a result of decisions other people are making.

Be prepared to be guided and to ask the kind of questions we set out earlier in the overview and then you need to make the decision with a full knowledge of the facts.

EXAMPLE OF COMBINATIONS IN UNIT 2

- Tom will perform a duologue for Section A with Clea.
- For Section B, Tom will perform in the group piece, under the direction of his teacher, while Clea has decided to go for the design option in Section B; she will look at costume design.
- In the same group, David will design the lighting for the duologue offered by Hope and Kirsty for Section A.
- In Section B, all three of these candidates will perform in the group piece under the direction of the teacher.
- Finally, in the same group, Theo has decided to offer design for both Section A and Section B.

12 Section A and B: performers

Now that we have looked at the overview of Unit 2 and you have made your decision to be a performance candidate, we need to look at more specific information about how you can access the marks in this unit against the assessment criteria.

This unit is about you:

- contributing to a group performance;
- contributing to a monologue or a duologue;
- experiencing the process of rehearsal;
- making interpretative decisions;
- experiencing performing to an audience.

Your teacher-director will lead you through the group performance and guide you towards your monologue or duologue with examination conditions in mind. The Edexcel specification clearly sets out the requirements for this Unit and tells us the following:

Texts should be chosen that offer students the opportunity to exhibit their acting or design skills that are the essential object of assessment. Centres should consider the skills, experience, and prior learning of candidates in choosing texts that will engage candidates' interest throughout the considerable preparation and rehearsal time needed for this unit.

The visiting examiner will assess your contribution to performance. The purpose of the preparation you will be involved in for this unit is to enable you to access the marks. Unit 2, Section B, for example, is not the school or college production or the audition piece (on the night of the examination) for the local drama festival. Your teacher may see this unit as a showcase opportunity for the Drama and Theatre Studies course, but the clear focus of the event itself has to be on the awarding of marks.

Unit 2 could have other knock-on effects for you. For those thinking of audition pieces during the final year of the course, preparing a monologue for Section A is an ideal preparation opportunity, but that is something for the future, not for the examination day itself.

Because the examination period for this unit stretches from February to May, it is likely that your teacher will be heavily involved in preparing you for the demands of Section B at the same time as you are preparing for Section A. As things stand at the time of writing, unless you are in a centre with more than nine candidates entering this examination, then both Section A and Section B will take place during the same examination session.

EXAMINATION SESSIONS EXPLAINED

An examination session is a period of time that an examiner might expect to spend in a centre assessing the work of students. For Unit 2, a session is up to three hours in length, and, during that time, up to nine students can be assessed for Section A and Section B.

If there are more than nine of you in your centre, then the examiner will expect to visit more than once. Your teacher will be aware of the requirements for this, but it may suit both you and your teacher, if numbers allow, for your examiner to visit on one day, during which you will present Section A and Section B over two examination sessions. On the other hand, again if numbers allow, it may be that your Section A is presented at the start of the examination series and your Section B towards the end of it. This is possible – as long as the examiner is able to visit more than once and is booked well enough in advance.

PREPARING FOR PERFORMANCE

This section gives some general thoughts on preparing yourself for performance in relation to the script and the work of practitioners who may have an influence on your ideas for both sections of this unit. First, you need to read the script so you know what it is about and how the information is presented by the playwright. There could be three stages to your reading at this point:

1. reading for information;
2. reading for understanding;
3. reading for actioning.

Once you have a reasonably secure idea about your choice or the role you have been given in the group piece, you may consider the following approach to preparing your monologue or duologue and your contribution to the group piece. It is always a good idea to make notes as you go along, preferably in pencil if these are going to be made in the body of the text itself. It is always good practice to have a pen and notebook ready next to you during rehearsals.

You may be given a photocopy of the extract for monologue or duologue which is fine as you start to develop your ideas around it; in fact, more than one copy will give you a chance to explore the development of your approach. You also need to have a complete copy of the play text too in order for you to be able to put your extract into its context which you will need to do for your rationale.

For Section B, your teacher may provide you with an edited version of the published play or you may spend a session putting the edits into clean copies of the script – either way, it is useful to be aware of what has been edited alongside what is to remain. An advantage of your teacher going through the script with you and collectively marking the edits is that he or she will probably talk you through the edits in relation to the concept as part of this process and you will have an early indication of the general approach to the text. Whether you are looking at Section A or Section B, you might find the following initial approach to the text useful.

Reading for information

Read the script and consider the following:

- What is the play about?
- How is the information presented by the playwright?
- How does your monologue or duologue fit into the whole?
- How does the role fit into the whole?

Reading for understanding

Make notes on the above and then read the script again, this time with more focus on the way the playwright develops the relationships between the characters and how this is presented to you in the script to aid your understanding as an actor.

- How is the dialogue presented?
- Are there words and phrases that leap out at you and help indicate particular aspects of character in relation to others?

Reading for actioning

Make notes on the previous section and look at ways of bringing the text to life for performance. Your focus is shifting at this point from the script as a whole to the section featuring your monologue or duologue and, for Section B, the scenes where your character appears. For this process to work, it is important that the background information gained so far not only informs your interpretation but also forms the basis for your written presentation for the examiner for Section A (and Section B if you are a design student).

After this initial three-stage approach to the text, you are now ready to apply your creative drama skills to the realisation of your role(s), your design option, or both. Your teacher may also advise you to look at the work of a practitioner alongside your preparation work here either because the choice of text warrants it or because they have a particular practitioner in mind in relation to the Section B text in performance. The following may help your understanding of the world of the practitioner.

PRACTITIONERS

Practitioners are great for helping you to access scripts and for exploring not only practical aspects of performance preparation but also some of the theory behind the practice.

You will have come across practitioners in exploring Unit 1, and those of you who have followed GCSE courses will probably have been introduced to at least one or two of the ideas of some of the people you will recognise at this level of study. There appears to be a circuit of practitioners who always seem to come round in examination drama, and there is a great familiarity at times in the ideas presented by students, particularly in written work. There is something refreshing for examiners and moderators in seeing new ideas being explored and unfamiliar names being mentioned as practitioners with influence over approaches to various aspects of exam work. It does not happen very often – and there is nothing to say that it must happen at all.

There is mention of practitioners elsewhere in this book but we have not produced an exhaustive list. What we are going to do in this section is look at what makes a practitioner and how ideas of some of the most often explored practitioners at this level of study may be utilised in exploring monologues, duologues and design considerations for Section A of Unit 2. This is presented with the understanding that you will have been through the Unit 1 exploration process by now and you will have looked at the work of at least one practitioner in relation to at least one of the Unit 1 texts; you will have notes about this practitioner that may be useful to you for Unit 2.

Our general definition is that a practitioner is a person or group of people whose ideas, methods, or approaches have made a significant contribution to the development of theatrical ideas and practices. This is usually seen on a national or international scale, and there is recognition from critics and existing practitioners of the influence of the work of others in this.

Consider the following three practitioners:

1. Katie Mitchell
2. Steven Berkoff
3. George Dillon.

Katie Mitchell

A clear example of making an impact can be seen in the work of director Katie Mitchell and her highly imaginative and controversial approach to, for example, classical texts, which is currently gaining her a reputation that could influence the work of others and establish theatre practice beyond her own directing. Her 2008 National Theatre production of *The Women of Troy*, for example, divided critics and audiences. More recently, her reimagining of Dostoyevsky's novel *The Idiot* as . . . *Some Trace of Her*, again at the National Theatre in London, invited audiences to question the nature of theatrical performance with its extensive use of video editing techniques and live projected images to focus and refocus her audience's responses, a technique she explored extremely effectively in her ground-breaking production of *Waves* in 2006/7.

The challenge in Mitchell's work is arguably in the telling of it, in her ability to look into the lives of her characters and to find techniques for assaulting the audience with fractured images that reform into the whole but, probably most importantly, the individual in the audience is confronted with his or her own version of the whole due to the nature of the performance itself.

Mitchell's work is presented at the National Theatre of England, and the debate it causes is reminiscent of the work of Steven Berkoff in the latter quarter of the twentieth century. (See also www.nationaltheatre.org.uk/platforms.)

Steven Berkoff

With Berkoff in mind, it is worth remembering that a number of well-known practitioners are also playwrights, but this is not always the case. The contribution of playwright as practitioner takes the work of the playwright beyond the content of the play and offers an approach or a series of approaches to the material within the script which can then be adapted to explore work by other playwrights. Berkoff's contribution to twentieth-century theatre has been well documented, not least by himself. He has developed and shaped an approach to **total theatre** that has been largely in relation to adaptations of classical texts, often in versions created by Berkoff himself – as writer, creator, director. Steven Berkoff immediately comes to mind when thinking about practitioners, but what is particularly interesting about Berkoff is that he is a good example of a practitioner and playwright of our times who is inspiring the next generation of practitioners in exploring and developing his particular approach to performance. (See also www.stevenberkoff.com.)

Total Theatre
Associated with Physical Theatre and arising from the work of, amongst others, Steven Berkoff. Total Theatre immerses the actor completely in the exploration of physical representation of character and situation.

George Dillon

One of the best known of the practitioners who have been inspired by Berkoff is George Dillon, some of whose work and ideas, with reference to his Vital Theatre Company can be found at www.georgedillon.com. George Dillon has worked with Berkoff and is in regular contact with him, exchanging ideas. In his own work he develops Berkoff's ideas in creating his own approaches and passing on his ideas to others in a way that both acknowledges the source and expands on it, redefining Berkoff's theatre for the twenty-first century. Dillon performs on a regular basis but he also spends time in schools and colleges working with students on developing a greater understanding of his approach to total theatre and, controversially, to his ideas on Berkoff's non-concept theatre.

Why practitioners are important

Practitioners are very helpful to us as they encourage us to understand the context of our contemporary theatre in relation to major developments in understanding how to explore its form and its impact upon a given audience. The dictionary definition of 'practitioner' is a person who practises a profession (think of a GP, general practitioner, for example), so, for our purposes, any person connected with the world of theatre could be seen as a practitioner. The definition has to be in place to narrow down the field but, as with everything else that is here, what follows is an example and there may be other more appropriate practitioners you or your teacher may wish to explore alongside this specification in order to enhance your work and your understanding of the wider theatrical context. Look at your Unit 1 work and practitioners there: your teacher must have chosen them for specific reasons in relation to the texts studied.

There is always an overlap of ideas and conventions. It is important to remember that nobody works in isolation in theatre and there is considerable overlap of ideas and theatrical movements, with refinements and modifications taking place over a number of years. The theatrical world in the twentieth century did not, for example, suddenly jump from Bertolt Brecht to John Osborne to Samuel Beckett to Harold Pinter to Steven Berkoff to Caryl Churchill. There was a natural process of evolution taking place which was part of the developments in theatre that have been going on since its very beginning. In the second half of the twentieth century, for example, it is very convenient to categorise theatre as pre- and post-1956. Whilst this is understandable, we must not lose sight of the developments taking place in the immediate post-Second World War period.

It is sometimes easier to talk in terms of specific movements and particular practices, which is perfectly acceptable, but it is always a good idea to have a sense of the context of the developments as well, recognising what else was going on while particular people were ploughing their own furrows and sowing a few seeds for others to pick up. The basic timeline at the start of this book gives you some ideas of the major movers and shakers in theatrical terms, many of whom still influence the work we do today.

It is very common for one practitioner to cite the influences of another and to recognise their own place within a wider developmental cycle – look at the Berkoff–Dillon relationship, for example.

Whilst looking at the work of specific practitioners, it is worth considering those who we no longer consider to be important and wonder why their influence was short-lived. Theatre history is littered with the casualties of shifting tastes and advancing ideas of what constitutes entertainment. For every playwright whose name we know, consider how many others there are who have disappeared into the dustbin of history.

Occasionally the work of some is rediscovered and lauded in lavish productions by one of our major companies, but, more often than not, the play and the playwright are then allowed to sink back into obscurity.

Tastes change, we know that ourselves just from everyday living. But selecting a monologue or duologue for an examination performance is not really about satisfying personal taste. We can recognise the theatrical worth in a piece without necessarily liking the piece itself.

WHERE ALL THIS FITS IN RELATION TO UNIT 2

Unit 2 is about is rising to the challenge of preparing an examination piece that will enable you to meet the criteria and, ultimately, achieve a mark that reflects your input and commitment to preparing the performance.

For the purposes of preparing for Unit 2, what we need to consider is the piece within its historical context and then apply appropriate rehearsal methods in order to explore it for performance, which may include reference to specific practitioners. On a very basic level, before you read the play, have a look within the text for any information there may be on the play itself and the playwright. Quite often a text will have a summary of the play (even if this is just on the back cover) and some information about its performance history and the playwright. Many texts have copious notes in them, depending on the edition you are looking at. Mostly these are extremely helpful but they do not necessarily need to influence your interpretation of your monologue or duologue. By placing the text within its historical context, you are recognising the content and the possible influences on the playwright at the time it was written. This information may or may not be helpful to you in your interpretation but before you can decide how helpful it may or may not be, you at least need to know and understand the context of the piece.

Plays are written to entertain and inform. Whilst some are undoubtedly more entertaining and informative than others, no playwright will set out deliberately to write a play that does not at the very least meet certain criteria in terms of content and possible audience perception. Whether the final piece entertains and informs is often a matter of taste, and there is no legislation to say that one person's triumph of the form will necessarily appeal to everybody. If there were a magic formula for this then theatre would be full of even more success stories than it already is instead of being littered with disasters and failures.

Our top five practitioners

Here is our list of our top five practitioners. Like everything else, this is not an exhaustive or exclusive list; it is merely an idea of where you might go in considering practitioners in relation to either your Section A piece or your Section B performance. Each name on the list has a distinct place in theatrical history, and two are still alive and currently practising.

Theatre of Cruelty

The theatre of Antonin Artaud. A forerunner of In Yer Face Theatre that challenges the audience on every level and sets out to make them think about the human condition. Artaud's use of the word 'cruelty' needs further exploration as it encompasses a range of ideas for performers and designers as well as audience.

1. **Edward Gordon Craig:** Notable for his ideas on stage design and the use of screens to shape and frame action on the stage, with his actors seen mainly as objects to be manipulated within the elaborate defining of spaces. Craig is still a major influence on theatre, particularly in relation to the use of light and defining spaces.

2. **Antonin Artaud:** Notable for his ideas around the **Theatre of Cruelty** which is an often misunderstood and misquoted term that covers a great deal of Artaud's work on challenging audiences and

wanting them to sit up and take notice of theatre, becoming actively involved rather than passively observing.

3. **Konstantin Stanislavsky:** A major influence on the actor in the twentieth century and a practitioner who is still very much at the fore-front of actor training today. You could not possibly step into a rehearsal space without coming across at least one technique developed by Stanislavsky, and you cannot study theatre without reference to his work.

4. **Max Stafford-Clarke:** Co-founder of Joint Stock Theatre Company, later Out of Joint, and developed a particular collaborative style of working with actors and writers to develop material before performance. Directed some major productions in the later years of the twentieth century, including a major double bill at the Royal Court theatre of *The Recruiting Officer* by George Farquhar and *Our Country's Good* by Timberlake Wertenbaker. He is still exerting an influence on theatre practice.

5. **Frantic Assembly:** Frantic Assembly produces thrilling, energetic and uncompromising theatre. The company makes work that reflects contemporary culture. In collaboration with a wide variety of artists, Frantic Assembly's artistic directors – Scott Graham and Steven Hoggett – create new work that places equal emphasis on movement, design, music and text. Since its formation in 1994, Frantic Assembly has toured extensively throughout the UK and abroad, building its reputation as one of the country's most exciting companies.

Extension Activity

Practitioners

In pairs, take one name from the list and prepare a short presentation lasting up to ten minutes for your group, detailing the major influences of your practitioner on the theatre world. You should take up to a week to research and prepare your presentation which should detail the major facts about the contribution your chosen practitioner has made to theatre practice. Consider our top five alongside this list of other practitioners:

- Steven Berkoff
- Augusto Boal
- Bertolt Brecht
- Peter Brook

- Théâtre de Complicité
- Jerzy Grotowski
- Kneehigh Theatre Company
- Jacques Lecoq
- Joan Littlewood
- Vsevolod Meyerhold

Depending on the size of your group, it may be that there is an opportunity for you to look at the work and impact of others from this list too. Be guided by your teacher on this but, certainly, if you are considering theatre design in this unit then you cannot do this really without considering the work of Edward Gordon Craig in particular.

PREPARING FOR SECTION A

There is a real need for you to think about commitment and time management in relation to preparing for this unit. What you do will not only have an effect on your marks, but could also influence your examiner's decisions about the marks of other in your group too. It is important that you adopt a mature and responsible approach to structuring your work. Your preparation may look like this:

- selecting
- preparing
- contextualising
- rehearsing
- structuring
- reflecting
- perfecting
- performing

This process will be helpful to you and to your teacher who does not need to be distracted from the whole process of preparing for Unit 2 by a student who cannot make a decision on the Section A choice or who is distracting or disruptive to others. Your teacher will set parameters in which you need to work and deadlines with milestones along the way, but it is very likely that preparation for Section A will be more student-driven than teacher-led.

This unit is all of those elements that go into creating an exciting and innovative piece of theatre, involving the development of a sense of company and the process of shaping and forming the final performances within the Exam Board guidelines and other supporting materials.

The individual skill

The individual skill is a challenge once you have decided what it is you are going to do. In this section, we are going to look at some possible ideas for monologues or duologues with suggestions for how you might approach the individual skill with the examiner in mind.

Essentials of a monologue

- Is it interesting enough on its own to engage my audience?
- Does it make sense away from its original context?
- Does it give me an opportunity to demonstrate a range of vocal skills appropriate to my interpretation of the extract?
- Is there opportunity for movement within my interpretation of the extract?
- Do I understand what the speech is about and how I should interpret it for my audience?

Essentials of a duologue

- Is it interesting enough on its own to engage my audience?
- Does it make sense away from its original context?
- Does it give me an opportunity to demonstrate a range of vocal skills appropriate to the extract in interaction with my partner?
- Is there opportunity for movement within our interpretation of the extract?
- Is there – more or less – a balance in the roles within the piece?
- Do we understand what the duologue is about and how we should interpret it for our audience?

The Examiner says:

It is probably a good idea, whether you choose monologue or duologue, to be careful about the timing of your piece. The suggested times are maximum times, not the starting point for the piece. Your examiner will not mark anything you present that is longer than the suggested time – so there is no point working on it and spending your time preparing it if it is not going to count towards your final mark.

Keep careful control over the timing of your piece and don't be tempted to add a little more. Whilst your examiner is unlikely to sit in front of you with a stop watch, he or she will note the time that you start and finish your performance. If it is significantly outside the allotted time, then the examiner will ignore material presented beyond the limit. There will be no exceptions to this so please be very aware of your timings when preparing your piece. It is a good idea to build time checks into your preparation. This may seem to suggest that the examiner is being 'harsh' in not responding to the material you are presenting. This is not the case – this is an examination, and our role is to ensure that the criteria are met for all candidates as far as we possibly can. There can be no exceptions to this, and you, as a candidate, need to know that your work is being assessed as far as is humanly possible in exactly the same way as a fellow candidate in another school or college.

Select a piece that is a little on the short side but that allows you an opportunity to incorporate some 'business' that will make up the time but that you can alter in terms of length if you find nearer the date of your performance that you need to do so.

The length of the piece is determined by what you do with it, not necessarily the time taken to read the lines on the page. Whilst care should be taken not to try to do too much, you need to consider that each of the assessment elements carries equal weighting so you need to demonstrate your approach to each of those elements in equal measure. Although you may, for example, find a particular physical challenge in the opening three or four lines of *Waiting for Godot* by Samuel Beckett, these three or four lines may not in themselves be enough for you and your partner to access the outstanding area for vocal skills and characterisation from the assessment grid. Be guided by your teacher on this – but consider all of the elements in the assessment grid before you make your final decision.

CHOOSING MY MONOLOGUE OR DUOLOGUE

Very simply, you need to decide what impact you want to have on your examiner and where your own particular strengths may lie in presenting your monologue or duologue. The following may help you.

Do I want to be:

* serious
* funny
* sad
* melodramatic
* demonstrative
* caring
* moving
* hilarious
* angry
* forceful
* responsive
* loud
* quiet
* engaging
* or a combination of two or more of the above?

The temptation is to choose a speech that will either attempt to be deadly serious or hilariously funny. It is an examination, after all, and we want you to make an impact on your examiner.

If something is funny, there is always the obvious sign of an audience response to look and listen for; you can tell if it is going well by the reaction of the audience. If something is serious, then you can expect silence as an appropriate reaction from your audience. The important thing is to choose a monologue or duologue that gives you the opportunity to show what you can do in a relatively short period of time in relation to the assessment criteria.

Be challenged – but be realistic.

There are clear challenges for you in an extract from *Decadence* by Steven Berkoff that would not be evident in an extract from *Blue Remembered Hills* by Dennis Potter, for example, not least of which would be coping with Berkoff's explicit exploration of sexual relationships in this particular play. Your judgement on this is not a judgement on the suitability of material for this level of study – although you and your teacher may feel that this may be an issue – it is about you and how comfortable you feel in exploring the character you are going to be portraying. A monologue or duologue leaves you pretty exposed out there so you need to be as sure as you possibly can be that the choice of material is right for you. There is reference in the specification to creating a monologue by omitting lines from another character in order for you to create a continuous speech. There is nothing wrong with this, but you need to approach this idea with caution and consult your teacher carefully before you set off to do this. An interjected line or two may have a major impact on your character at that particular moment and to cut the lines in order for you to create a monologue may not always be ideal for your purpose. It is probably not a good idea to create a monologue for a character by stringing together speeches or parts of speeches from various scenes in the play to create a new speech. The examiner is looking for you to present a monologue or duologue that is coherent and which reflects the complete play text. Have a look at this next section as a guide to help you think about your monologue or duologue, not as a suggested list of extracts you might want to consider.

EXPLORING THE MONOLOGUE OR DUOLOGUE

The extracts presented here are presented without contextualisation and are used to give you some ideas for how you might approach monologue or duologue for Section A. What you have is a series of approaches to a range of monologues and duologues, but the final choice has to be between you and your teacher.

What we have done is give you a range of possibilities for monologues and duologues from plays you may have heard of or you may even have studied for Unit 1. There is nothing prescriptive in the ideas here but as with everything in this book you may want to use our thoughts as a starting point and adapt them to suit your own approach to preparing for performance. A word of caution though if you are going to respond to one of our ideas here: you are not allowed to present a monologue or duologue from a text that you have already studied for Unit 1. The other thing you need to consider at this point is that the extracts presented here may or may not be of suitable length for Section A, so, as with your own choice of monologue of duologue, it is worth going back to the original script and looking at the extract in context in order to gain a fuller understanding of it and how long it might last in performance. You will need to find the original script in any case in order to access our extracts – and in the reading of it you may well find other more suitable material that you want to explore within the script.

When you find the extract from *4:48 Psychosis* by Sarah Kane, for example, you will see that it appears to be very short but, in performance, there may be opportunities to develop the piece to meet the time requirement and to enable a performance of the speech to reflect its context.

There is a mix of male and female characters in our choice of extracts. Edexcel has no issue with cross-gender casting in any performance work but it is very important to ask yourself the reasons why you want to explore a character of the opposite sex for this section and, if appropriate, for the unit as a whole.

There is a fantastic piece entitled *Man to Man* by Manfred Karge. It is based on a true story and is about a woman who assumes her husband's identity when he dies in order to keep working and earning a living for herself. It is a monologue and may be worth exploring if you feel the need for a cross-gender piece written to be performed in this way – Tilda Swinton created the role originally in 1992. There are major considerations you need to explore before deciding if it is right and appropriate, and your teacher is the first person you should turn to for advice on this. The examiner will mark your performance against the criteria, and there is nothing specific in the performance criteria that recognises your portrayal of somebody of the opposite sex.

Something that appears to cause most concern with monologues is the question of who to address during the delivery. Sometimes it is very clear that the character is talking to 'the audience' or is delivering inner thoughts and therefore has a different focus for the delivery. Monologue 3 from *Playhouse Creatures*, for example, indicates the focus is the husband of the speaker and he is 'in the auditorium'. The Old Man in *Two* by Jim Cartwright is clearly addressing the audience, indicated by his opening word: 'Howdo.'

It could be that your monologue is addressed to an object – a chair or hat stand, for example – during rehearsal, and this may also help you to focus and give direction to your speech. It is certainly worth borrowing a fellow group member to be a silent partner in rehearsal (this could, of course, be your critical friend), and it will be worth your teacher sounding out the examiner before the day of the performance just to double-check on what is acceptable from the Exam Board. It is highly likely that a monologue will have to be performed in the space, on your own with no silent partner or object to address to act as a focal point for your delivery. With this in mind, you should probably consider moving your rehearsal forward at a steady pace to enable you to think of the focus of your delivery without the aid of a fellow student or object to address. You may find that a prop or a piece of costume will be useful to you in helping you to develop your character, and this is perfectly acceptable for you to use during the performance. A packet of mints to take away the bitter taste of Creon's words to Antigone in the play of the same name, or a sword for Henry V could be very useful, or example.

The specification has introduced this section to this unit to give you an opportunity to demonstrate your developing understanding of creating a performance within a given context, and there are ways of doing this that will meet the requirements of the specification.

Direct address to the examiner could be a little tricky as the examiner has a job to do and may not feel comfortable being part of your performance to such an extent that the purpose of the delivery becomes secondary. Your examiner has two minutes maximum to consider your performance against the criteria and, therefore, may not wish to be distracted from that task.

It may or may not be appropriate therefore to deliver your monologue directly to the examiner. It all depends on the context of the speech and your interpretation of it, but there is certainly nothing written within the specification to indicate that you must address the examiner directly with your monologue or, indeed, that you must not.

'Is this a dagger which I see before me, the handle toward my hand?', for example, probably does not require you to look directly at the examiner and wait for a nod of affirmation or a shake of the head before continuing with the speech. What it might require, however, is a point of focus within your acting space in which the vision of the dagger appears to Macbeth, and this point of focus may, initially, be in the general direction of the examiner or in the downstage area if you are presenting in a more formal setting. Clearly your preparation process will take into account not only the 'what' of your monologue but also the 'where', and there are things you can do to make sure that your presentation is performed as confidently as possible. Focus is extremely important in delivering, particularly, the monologue. By the very nature of the task you are there on your own, exposed.

Think about it:

- What do you do with your hands?
- Where do you stand?
- When do you move?
- Where do you look?

This is not a simple task, and you need to be prepared to work hard on it if you want to be able to access the marks at the higher level. One of the key preparation techniques you can adopt is to explore the focus of the piece and where you, as actor, could direct your attention during the delivery. There is nothing worse than 'wandering eyes' during delivery, and this is something that any examiner will be looking for in any performance across this unit. 'Wandering eyes' coupled with 'shuffling feet' are a recipe for major disaster in performance, and part of being confident and comfortable with your performance is having a clear understanding of how you present yourself to the audience. There is a fine line between coming across to the examiner as mechanical, technically competent and in control of the piece, and presenting the character physically in an engaging way. The preparation process is to be decided between you and your teacher, but, as with a lot of performance preparation, it is probably a good idea to start with mechanical, and then, as you become more aware of the character within the piece and how your interpretation is reflecting this, tone this down and adapt it towards

Figure 12.1
How a student may perform a monologue before the examiner.

Source: Alan Perks and Jacqueline Porteous.

a more 'naturalistic' representation within the context of your interpretation. Have a go now with one of the extracts and see how you react to the character and what you can bring to the performance that makes you feel comfortable in exploring the role – or not. At this stage in your preparations, you have nothing to lose, but the final decision about Section A has to be between you and your teacher, and it is really important that you consider all possibilities before making that decision. What follows is not an exhaustive list but you can apply the following approaches to any extract you feel may be appropriate for this section. It is important that you are able to contextualise the extract within the play as a whole – an exploration of 'to be, or not to be' is a different challenge from any of the following extracts, not least because of the length of the complete play itself. Moreover, it is important to remember at this point that you do need to demonstrate an understanding of the complete play in your concept. You will need to look up the following extracts in their original context – but we would be surprised if most if not all of the texts are not available in either your Drama Department or in the school or college resources centre. The advantage of this for you is that you will also get a feel for the extract in its setting, particularly for those with which you are less familiar. You will need to carry out this kind of activity in the reality of Unit 2 Section A.

Have your notebook ready – off you go.

Extension Activity

Exploring a monologue or duologue

Choose a monologue and/or duologue of your own and prepare it for the group. When you feel that it is ready, share it with your group and discuss your interpretation. An extract from one of your Unit 1 texts may lend itself to this activity, or you may have seen or read something that really engaged and inspired you and want to share it with others before deciding on it for your own performance piece. It will not take long for you to build up a bank of monologues or duologues that may be of use to you in the future. Use the timeline in the book to look at specific periods of theatrical development and see what there is in plays from those time periods that may lend themselves to exploring monologues/duologues. On a simple level, you may look at:

- Greek;
- medieval;
- sixteenth or seventeenth century;
- eighteenth or nineteenth century;
- twentieth century;
- twenty-first century.

As well as supporting your work in this unit, you are also exploring possibilities for possible future audition pieces and giving yourself an opportunity for extending your knowledge and understanding of different theatrical styles.

MONOLOGUES

1. 'Old Man' from *Two* by Jim Cartwright

Two by Jim Cartwright is a rich source of monologues (and duologues), offering as it does a series of male and female characters during one night in a pub in the North of England. *Two* is designed so that two people can play all the characters. From: Old Man: Howdo. (sups beer)

One of the first things to look at in relation to this monologue is the dialect. We know that the character is from a play set in the North of England, and this may influence any interpretation of the character in your monologue. You need to consider the importance of the dialect to the character. Ask yourself two questions:

1. Is it acceptable to look for another regional dialect in order to interpret the character?
2. Is 'Old Man' purely a Northern character, or is there universality about his monologue that will transfer to any location in an interpretation of him?

Look at who the character is. A major piece of information is in his name: 'Old Man'. Where is he, and what is he doing? Look at the who, where and why of the character.

- Who is he? An old man.
- Where is he? In a pub with a pint of beer.
- Why is he there? To tell us about his feelings for his dead wife who is always with him in his thoughts.

Look now at the way the speech is set out on the page. It has been reproduced here in more or less the same way as it is set out in the published version of the play. Look at the pauses in the speech. Some of these are connected to his drinking, but not all, some of them are to signify a memory or thought about his wife.

The speech is divided into short bursts, and this could be both good and bad for a monologue. If the pauses are too long in performance, then you are in danger of losing the flow of the piece, but if the pauses are too short then they will lose their purpose and it could appear as though you are losing the thread of the performance because you are rushing it.

Read it aloud and try to get some sense of the flow of the speech with the dialect in place as far as possible. Consider the tone of the delivery and clues for this are in the lines themselves. There are wistful, longing moments, and there are moments of resignation too. Decide how you might approach this speech if you were going to attempt it for your monologue.

What skills would you need in order to action it? Are there qualities within the speech that will take you outside your own experience and give you an appropriate challenge for this level of study?

Does it need to be 'Old Man'? Probably, yes, it does in this instance – but you may have a take on it that will develop the character effectively as Old Woman. Reassigning characters is always worth consideration, but listen to your teacher on this one – some times it is more appropriate than others, and this particular play has an interesting range of characters, both male and female, so the need to play the Old Man cross-gender or to change him to Old Woman should not really be necessary as there are plenty of other characters who you could play appropriately without having to change the sex of this one.

Extension Activity

Exploring Old Man

- What else could you do to develop an approach to this character?
- Create three practical activities that could help somebody else in your group to explore this character.
- Write a character study of Old Man based on the information you have here in this extract.
- Annotate the extract as if you were preparing it for performance. What would you need to include in your annotation?
- Choose a different extract from the same text – either on your own or with a partner – and prepare it for performance.

2. 'When sanity visits', from *4:48 Psychosis* by Sarah Kane

From: At 4:48 when sanity visits.

There are challenges in this speech, not least of which is the stream-of-consciousness nature of it. Look at how the speech is set out on the page in the published edition of the play. This is, presumably, as Sarah Kane intended it to be set out. There is some indication that this speech was written for one person with two interjections at the end of it indicated by '–'. The Royal Court production of the play featured three actors – two female and one male – but this speech appears to work as a complete piece for one actor, with the interjections possibly interpreted as inner thoughts, questioning the logic of the speech. It is not an easy speech, but it could be very rewarding, particularly in the context of the whole play and in relation to the demands of the unit. Getting the tone right is very important with this speech. There may be a temptation to be either too demonstrative or too introspective, neither of which would necessarily enable you to access the full range of marks here, and both interpretations could demonstrate a shallow understanding of Sarah Kane's intentions. Applying the who, where and why process here is essential as you look to unravel the complexities of the role that are presented here by Kane. Something you will need to consider carefully is the length of the piece and how you might explore this within the context of this section. A maximum of two minutes does not appear to be a lot but sometimes it can seem forever when you are struggling to fill the time. It may be interesting to explore this monologue as a duologue and see how you might divide the lines to offer opportunities for more than one voice. This kind of script allows for a number of approaches, all of which are valid in terms of performance but you must be clear in your own mind that an interpretation would be valid for the assessment criteria for this unit.

Extension Activity

Exploring challenging monologues

- Look at other sections of *4:48 Psychosis* and explore them with the requirements of this section in mind. You could look at these sections as either monologues or duologues.
- Look at *Requiem for Ground Zero* by Steven Berkoff – the opening page will give you a flavour of it – and consider how you might present this as a monologue. Some of Berkoff's other work is worth exploring with this section in mind too, not only his monologues but also some of his other scripts contain great monologue opportunities – look at Sylv in *West,* for example.

3. 'Mrs Betterton', from *Playhouse Creatures* by April De Angelis

From: Scene 2: Mrs Betterton comes forward, and addresses Mr Betterton who is unseen in the auditorium.

An interesting aspect of this monologue is that it was written to include unheard responses to Mrs Betterton from her husband. In performance, it is assumed that 'Mr Betterton' is present, and this would therefore give a focus for the performance of the speech. Mrs Betterton will presumably move within the space and probably address a static Mr Betterton in the auditorium. It might be worth exploring this a little, however, and have her search him out as he wanders in the space beyond the stage and somewhere within your audience.

This speech on first reading may appear a little more complex than it is. Build in the pauses for the responses from Mr Betterton to give more of a sense of the flow of the speech. Applying the who, where and why approach will help you in considering the role in its wider context and how you might develop Mrs Betterton within this extract.

There is a theatricality to the character that is worth exploring and a real sense of purpose in the exchange which has opportunities for exploring humour with an eye on the pauses and how they could be handled.

Extension Activity

Exploring the context

- What do you learn about Mrs Betterton just from this extract?
- What do you learn about Mr Betterton?
- Research the context of the play and make notes on what you think it says about theatre in the time period in which it is set.
- If you are thinking of offering design for this section, consider costume for Mrs Betterton and research possible costume ideas to reflect the time period.

4. 'Liz', from *Our Country's Good* by Timberlake Wertenbaker

From: Act II, Scene 1, Visiting Hours. (Liz, Wisehammer, Arscott, Caesar all in chains. Arscott is bent over facing away.)

In terms of the challenge of exploring language and specifically slang, this speech is the most complicated one here.

Lizzie Morden, a convict in a colony in Australia in the eighteenth century is telling us of her childhood, her relationship with her father and brother and how she came to be caught red-handed and deported for pickpocketing.

The speech is not an easy one, but it has its own rewards in the rich playing with the language of the character and the confidence you could bring in delivery to indicate your understanding of the character and what she has been through to get to this point in her story.

This is the start of Act II, presumably following an interval, and the speech introduces the audience to the characters behind bars. Liz is telling her fellow convicts about how she came to be deported, and, in doing so, she is also telling the audience something about the judicial system of the time. The who, where and why of the character is reasonably straightforward, and there is a lot of historical reference to this character outside Wertenbaker's text. It is not essential that you research beyond the text but you might find it interesting to have a look at other historical references in relation to Lizzie as part of your background to developing the role.

A starting point for this kind of heavily colloquial speech is to try to read it with a real sense of purpose initially, getting a feel for the pattern of the speech before worrying about the meaning of all of the words. Some words will become more obvious as you read them and there is enough of an implication from others that it becomes easier to get a sense of their meaning. There are real challenges here, some of which will be answered by research into the character and the time period, others which you will address in your interpretation. What you must not do is be immediately put off by this speech because it is not at first as accessible as some of the others.

5. 'The First Man', from *The Tin Can People* by Edward Bond

From: (The FIRST MAN comes on.)

To: (The FIRST WOMAN comes on.)

This speech is from the opening of the play and establishes the character and situation for the audience. The play itself is relatively short and forms part of *The War Plays* trilogy from Edward Bond. It is set in a post-apocalyptic world in which the survivors are starting to recreate some semblance of primitive society in which tinned food (i.e. uncontaminated food) becomes vital for their survival.

The characters are not given names; they are, for example, First Man and Second Woman, and they represent types rather than individuals. It is a bleak play, but not without humour, and this speech effectively switches between the ramblings of somebody who is used to talking aloud to himself and the immediate focus on the tin can and its potential for aiding survival. There is a nervous energy to the speech, almost an opportunity to couple disjointed movements with the disjointed nature of the delivery. Like the 'Liz' speech from *Our Country's Good,* there is a real challenge here in not only delivering the monologue but also in making sense of Bond's phrasing and jumbled imagery for this character at this moment in the play.

Look at the first instruction: *'he groans mechanically'*. Here is your first challenge as actor preparing this speech. We can understand the groan, but why 'mechanically'? Is it because it is an automatic response to the condition he finds himself in? Is it to give the audience time to adjust to the appearance of this figure? Or is it a lead into the first line about the organ-grinder that rises from the mechanical groan?

Consider the who, where and why of the character and the fact that we have here the opening speech of the play and an introduction for the audience of something of what is to come as the play unfolds. You might consider reading *The Road* by Cormac McCarthy as part of your research into this role.

Extension Activity

Exploring the war plays of Edward Bond

- Read the plays in this collection that make up *The War Plays*. What vision of the world is Bond giving us in this collection?
- How does this vision fit in with what you know about him as a playwright?
- You know very little? Find out more, as Edward Bond is credited with bringing about a major change in British theatre in the late twentieth century.
- What is this change – and how do you think it is still influencing your work today?

DUOLOGUES

1. 'Brenda and Carol' from *Road* by Jim Cartwright

From: The lights come up on another living room. An old beaten red arm-chair, an ironing-board up at the back. Brenda, a thin wizened scruffy woman, sits in the chair facing the audience, smoking. At the back, Carol, in bra and knickers, is ironing her dress. Brenda: (speaks in a low, quiet, one-tone voice) Where you goin'?

To: Brenda: Ask men.

No apologies for another Jim Cartwright extract in this section. If you are looking for a monologue or a duologue from a late twentieth-century play that has bite and social commentary, then Jim Cartwright needs consideration. He is not the only playwright who fits the bill – others are mentioned elsewhere – but he does have a way with the language that encourages attention from the audience – and this extract is a prime example of that. These two women cannot be ignored.

This is the first time we meet Brenda and Carol in the play. They are mother and daughter and present a real challenge to you in terms of staying on the right side of exaggeration in your portrayal of them. They are probably not like any other mother and daughter you may have come across so far, and there lies the challenge. They are appalling, yet fascinating – a fantastic combination for this unit and for this exercise in particular. Hit your audience with Brenda and Carol, and they will stay hit! Impact is guaranteed – if you do your work properly and get the flavour of these two just right. There are no half measures here. What you see with these two should be what your audience gets.

Consider the who, where and why of Brenda and Carol and then play with the characters within the overall context of the play. There is great fun to be had in the repetition within the extract and some excellent descriptive phrasing. It may be an idea as part of your preparation process to change roles with your partner more than once and to get a real feel for which role is better suited to each of you. Try this in your exploration of this extract if you do have a go at it. There is very little to choose between the two characters here but you need to keep reminding yourself that Brenda is Carol's mother, and that should help contextualise the piece for you. You may wish to look at this mother–daughter relationship alongside that of Faith and Evelyn in Duologue 5 from *Kindertransport* by Diane Samuels. An interesting approach to the extract could be to consider that Brenda enjoys these heated exchanges with her daughter and that everything she says is designed to wind Carol up – it is all calculated and controlled by Brenda, and Carol falls for it every time.

What does the exchange tell us about the characters and their relationship? Where are the challenges for you and your partner in exploring Carol and Brenda?

2. 'Vladimir and Estragon', from *Waiting for Godot* by Samuel Beckett

From: (The light suddenly fails. In a moment it is night. The moon rises at back, mounts in the sky, stands still, shedding a pale light on the scene)
To: (They do not move.) CURTAIN.

This duologue is from the play of which it has been said 'nothing happens – twice'. Arguably, *Waiting for Godot* is one of the most influential plays of the twentieth century, and this exchange between the two central characters is typical of the piece, in both tone and content.

There is an awful lot happening here in terms of the relationship, and this extract builds effectively to the anti-climatic moment that ends the play. There is no doubt that there is affection in this relationship that transcends moments of tension between the two characters. There is nothing that will separate them now.

There are three things you might need to consider as you look at this extract:

1. Samuel Beckett was a big fan of silent movies – particularly the films of Charlie Chaplin and Laurel and Hardy and that kind of knockabout, slapstick humour.
2. Beckett always insisted that his characters only lived in the confines of the play, and any talk of pre- or after-life in a Stanislavskian approach to characterisation was dismissed by him. That does not mean we have to dismiss it now, but it does give us some idea about the playwright's intentions in relation to this text as a whole. It is a classic example of absurd theatre – and any approach will need to recognise and understand what is meant by this.
3. Beckett would not have approved of his characters being played by female actors. Again, this does not mean that you should not do this but it does, again, give you an idea of his thinking behind the characters and their relationship.

Applying the who, where and why approach to the characters of Vladimir and Estragon is particularly interesting, especially if you think that they are interchangeable or that there is little difference between them. There are clues within this extract, but these are, of course, developed much further within the text as a whole.

Extension Activity

Exploring Theatre of the Absurd

*   Find out why *Waiting for Godot* is considered to be such an important play. Use Martin Esslin's *Theatre of the Absurd* as a source of information.

- Was *Waiting for Godot* greeted with universal praise during its first run? Why might this have been the case?
- Why do you think it is still performed today and is regarded as a classic of the genre?

3. 'Macbeth and Lady Macbeth', from *Macbeth* by William Shakespeare

From Act II, Scene 2: Lady Macbeth Enters, Lady: That which hath made them drunk hath made me bold;

To: Macbeth: Wake Duncan with thy knocking! I would thou couldst! (Exeunt)

The most murderous husband-and-wife team in theatrical history. A real opportunity here to let your acting skills have full reign in exploring the aftermath of the murder of Duncan and the shift in dominance in the relationship at this point. Lady Macbeth has persuaded Macbeth to carry out the deed, and it is now up to her to pick up the pieces as he appears in a state of shock at his own actions. Don't be put off by the language. There is nothing to be scared of here. There is a flow and a rhythm to this exchange that give it a life of its own. Macbeth has killed Duncan as Lady Macbeth encouraged him to do; they both must now face the consequences and prepare for the discovery of the body. If anything, this particular extract appears to be a little longer than the five minutes allowed, but it will cut and edit without making too much of a loss to the sense of it, and, as an exercise in itself, it is worth exploring from that point of view if nothing else. Caution is advised in this process as you still need to have a coherent duologue from the original, and you need to ensure that there is still a balance for your two performers in the editing. It may, of course, not be too long in your own interpretation of it but consider savouring the exchange and look at it as more of a three-course meal than a trip to the local fast-food outlet. As a playwright, Shakespeare lends himself beautifully to this section of Unit 2. There are hundreds of great speeches – both monologues and duologues – any of which could engage and entrance your audience and earn you high marks in this section if you put the work in. Shakespeare was not adverse to cross-gender casting either!

A word of caution though: this section of Unit 2 is not just about preparing your monologue, duologue or design element, but is also about demonstrating your decisions in relation to the play as a whole.

You need to think smart about this: as we have already indicated, the mark scheme is the same whether you are performing a speech from *Hamlet* or a speech from *Blue Remembered Hills*. We are not making a value judgement here, but what we are doing is, we hope, to have you think a little about the purpose of the exercise. Your task is not only to present your chosen piece to the examiner but also to contextualise it in your written rationale. Shakespeare is great and completely accessible for this section but you need to choose wisely.

Consider the who, where and why of this exchange – many of you will be familiar with the plot of the play already – and then look at the relationship between these two characters. There is a lot going on that you and your partner should really enjoy bringing out for your audience. There are challenges that have to be met, but the where and why should help you in this – particularly if you reference the fact that they have between them just committed murder, it is the middle of the night, and neither of them wishes to be discovered.

This is the kind of extract that you might want to explore by taking away the language and creating a silent-movie version of the scene with appropriately exaggerated gestures and movements. Add captions from the original dialogue at moments you feel important and develop the captions into longer speeches from the original text as you become more confident about the language in relation to the movement. It is a highly charged moment from the play and should give you both the chance to really explore this relationship at this point. A design-skills candidate working with you could also have a field day on any of the available skills with, perhaps, the exception of mask.

Extension Activity

Exploring the Porter

*   Look at the Porter's speech from *Macbeth* and create a monologue that brings out the intended humour in it. Share your monologue with the group.

4. 'Meg and Stanley', from *The Birthday Party* by Harold Pinter

From: The Street door slams. STANLEY returns.

To: (Silence. He groans, his trunk falls forward, his head falls into his hands)

Beneath the façade of suburban respectability, nothing is as it first appears. This is Harold Pinter at his most intriguing as Meg introduces to Stanley, her lodger, the idea of the impending arrival of the 'two gentlemen'.

There is a clear hint of a relationship between Meg and Stanley, certainly from her point of view, and this relationship needs to be explored during the duologue as it is key to Stanley trying – but failing – to gain the upper hand towards the end of the exchange.

Do not be fooled by the apparent simplicity of this exchange or its context. When you read the whole text you will see the steadily unfolding menace that is hinted at here, and, in doing so, you will probably find other potential duologues that will lend themselves beautifully to this section. Pinter is arguably the master of the unspoken, and there is a real challenge in bringing to life these characters from one of his earlier plays. Grouped into the category of the 'Theatre of the Absurd', Pinter is recognised particularly for the use of pause and for the underlying feeling of menace and contained violence present in much of his work. On exploring this particular exchange, you and your partner need to consider this relationship along similar lines to the relationship between Macbeth and Lady Macbeth in Duologue 3, certainly with regard to dominance.

It might also be a useful exercise to connect Beckett and Pinter and to look at a wider approach to Theatre of the Absurd through these extracts here in order to help with an understanding of the meaning of the term.

By applying the who, where and why approach to this extract, you are considering a seemingly naturalistic domestic setting in relation to an exchange that becomes increasingly more complex as the scene develops. The setting is a lodging house, familiar to audiences of the day but perhaps less so in the twenty-first century. This may influence your contextualisation of the scene and help you to decide whether to update the setting or to leave it as a period piece – either decision will have implications for your interpretation of the roles.

Extension Activity

Exploring your concept

- Write notes for your concept as if you were going to prepare this extract for performance.
- Look at the requirements for a concept and detail what you may include based on the criteria and this extract in order to earn a mark in the outstanding box from your examiner.

5. 'Faith and Evelyn', from *Kindertransport* by Diane Samuels

From: (A key jangles in the door lock. The door opens. Evelyn enters. She carries a tea towel. If she sees Helga and Eva, even momentarily, she ignores them. She is followed by Faith.) Evelyn: Most of it is junk.

To: Evelyn: You'll need something to drink from in your new home. (Evelyn continues to polish. Faith, helpless, watches)

Evelyn and her daughter Faith search the attic for anything that may be of use to Faith as she prepares to set up her new home (again). There is a brittleness about the exchange, something below the surface that is not expressed at this point by either character and a real challenge for you in exploring and performing, with a lot of opportunity to create an attic space in which to present these two characters. This is the first time we meet these two characters in the play, and the relationship is defined very effectively at key moments during this exchange.

It is perhaps a little too long for the examination – depending on how effectively you explore the pauses – but there is room within it for edits in order to bring it in line with the published time requirement of a maximum of five minutes for the duologue. When you read the text as a whole you will see that there are particular challenges in the structure of this play and in the time shifts that happen regularly within scenes. This is the first time we have met Evelyn, for example, but we have already met her younger self in an exchange with her birth mother preparing for 'Eva' to be evacuated from Germany in 1938 to escape the rise of Nazism. At this stage in the play, Faith is not aware of her mother's past, but it is a very neat structure by Diane Samuels to have two mother–daughter preparations for departure to open the play. There are also a number of other duologue opportunities within the text, some of which may take you across the time periods if, for example, there are interesting possibilities if you explore the character of 'Lil', Evelyn/Eva's adoptive mother.

As far as this duologue is concerned, it is useful to apply the who, where and why approach, particularly when you consider the structure of the play as a whole. You will see that your interpretation of this scene although set in the 'present' needs to be a 'present' that is realistic in terms of the childhood of Eva in the 1930s: the early 1980s fits the timescale for this.

It may also be useful to explore this mother–daughter exchange alongside Brenda and Carol from *Road* (Duologue 1), which would be an interesting and challenging exercise in itself.

Five minutes for your duologue is not long. In exploring this extract from *Kindertransport,* if you had to edit it to fit the time limit, what would you edit and why?

MAKING THE CHOICE: THE PROCESS

Now that you have been able to have a look at a number of ideas for monologue and duologues, you need to think about where this is going to take you. Have a look at the assessment criteria again and see what the examiner will be looking for in your monologue or duologue on the day. In your performance, you will be assessed on your skills in relation to:

- vocal (clarity, use of pause, pace, pitch, tone inflection and projection);
- movement (the ability to use gesture, poise and stillness with control and sensitivity);
- characterisation (understanding of the role and its context within the play).

Your choice of monologue or duologue must allow you to access the marks in these three areas as well as for your concept notes as set out in the specification. This process will be different for different people. Possible routes could be:

- You may be given a collection of monologues and duologues and asked to read through them to find one that you think may be suitable before you read the whole play to find its context for your written concept.
- You may decide to explore some of the monologues and duologues in this book, and these may inspire you to look at one of these or other potential extracts by the same playwrights – or to avoid them at all costs!
- You may know a particular play already. This may be something you have seen or something you have performed in or studied. Remember though that this cannot be a text you have already explored for Unit 1, although there is nothing to stop you choosing a monologue or duologue from a different play by one of your Unit 1 playwrights.
- You may simply have heard of a play or a character and want to find out more in order to see if the script offers any opportunities for this unit.

Whatever the process, some of you will have more freedom of choice here than others. It is likely that teachers will vary in their approach to this, and some may have a small selection of ideas for you to choose from. The advantage of this is that your teacher will have a greater knowledge of the scripts selected and will be able to guide you more effectively in the process. The disadvantage is that your choice will be more limited. Before you feel aggrieved if this is the case where you are, weigh this up and consider why your teacher is limiting your choice and what that will do for your potential to be guided more successfully towards accessing the marks. Sometimes too much choice is worse than no choice at all.

Your teacher may make the choice of Section A monologues or duologues based on the choice of script for Section B. A good example of this could be selections from *Two* by Jim Cartwright for Section A and his play *Road* for Section B. Other playwright combinations could be:

Table 12.1 *Possible play choices to link Section A with Section B*

Section A	Playwright	Section B
Requiem for Ground Zero	Steven Berkoff	*West*
The Tin Can People	Edward Bond	*The Sea*
Mother Courage	Bertolt Brecht	*The Caucasian Chalk Circle*
Vinegar Tom	Caryl Churchill	*Fen*
Bouncers	John Godber	*Teechers*
The Caretaker	Harold Pinter	*Mountain Language*
Hamlet	William Shakespeare	*Macbeth*
Oedipus	Sophocles	*Antigone*
The Love of a Nightingale	Timberlake Wertenbaker	*Our Country's Good*

Other combinations are there to be explored but there is no requirement at all to perform in plays by the same playwright in Section A and Section B. It is simply another way for your teacher to look at this unit and the experience you will have in performing it and your examiner and audience will have in watching it. Your teacher for example, may look at Greek theatre for Section A with monologues or duologues from *Antigone* by Sophocles and work on *Antigone* by Anouilh with the group for Section B. Another similar possibility could be Shakespeare's *Hamlet* for Section A and *A Midsummer Night's Dream* for Section B. Both of these possibilities are not only acceptable for this unit but they also look forward to the A2 year and Unit 4, sowing the seeds of research for both Elizabethan and Greek theatre. You are looking not only to have a wide and diverse experience in this subject but also to achieve a high grade – and any way of enabling you to do this has to be good.

Whatever the approach, spare a thought for your teacher at this time. Not only is Section A getting under way but Section B is under consideration too, and both sections have to be ready for examination within the same time period (although, as we have previously mentioned, there may be some flexibility in this depending on your numbers) and possibly on the same day, again depending on numbers in your centre.

A SAMPLE GROUP OF TWELVE

If you are in a group of twelve, then your teacher has to make sure that twelve Section A presentations are ready as well as probably two performance pieces for Section B. And by 'ready', we do not mean 'ready' for the day the examiner is coming but ready at least seven days before the examiner's visit because that is when all the forms, scripts and your production notes or concepts have to be sent off. There will inevitably be fine-tuning taking place in the final seven days before the examiner's visit, but all major decisions for Section A and for Section B will have been made by this stage as there should be no negative surprises for either the examiner or you and your teacher on the day of the examination. A group of twelve will be enough to warrant more than one visit from an examiner, but it is probably a good idea to assume the time scale for preparation and visits will probably preclude a long drawn-out process for this unit over weeks in the vast majority of cases. It is likely to be over days, and, whatever the agreed performance timetable, somebody will have to go first – and it is always best to assume that it is going to be you. A group of twelve, for example, is enough to require two visits from your examiner, but these two visits could be two sessions on the same day if it suits you, your teacher and your examiner to do this.

A useful tip at this point is to create a calendar of events leading *backwards* from the day(s) agreed for the examination to take place. Once that decision has been made and agreed, look at the steps that need to be taken in relation to that. Use the table that follows as a rough guide to creating your own countdown calendar.

Table 12.2 *Countdown calendar for Unit 2 examinations*

Date	What	Who	Checklist	Completed
April 15th	Examiner booked	All Groups	Performances ready – A and B.	
April 14th	Dress Rehearsal with audience	All Section B performances	JT and SB design presentations prepared and shared.	
April 10th	Presentation of Section A pieces in order	All Section A pieces	Performances ready.	
April 5th	Send all documentation to examiner	Double check all concepts and extracts	Dress and Tech run period 4 and 5.	

Table 12.2 *continued*

Date	What	Who	Checklist	Completed
April 1st ...	All Section A concepts in for checking – final version prepared under supervised conditions	Check annotated extracts for all	Check timings and running order to allow for two design presentations. Revise concepts with all – do they still make sense? Talk through with everybody about their concept again before they are sent off. Discuss the importance of the concepts, check notebooks and prepare for the final versions.	

GO FOR THE CHALLENGE

The most important thing to remember is that it is you who will be performing for the examiner, and, therefore, you need to feel comfortable with the material. This does not mean that you necessarily go for an easy option. It is good to be challenged by a character and his or her circumstances and to have to really work to find a way of engaging with a complex personality.

Challenge at this level of study is always a good idea and enables you to look at the broader context of your work in relation to study beyond A-Level. The broader the experience you can offer, the more likely you are to be able to take your interests further if that is what you wish to do.

The Examiner says:

As we have previously mentioned – but it is worth repeating – there is no such thing as a 'suitable' text for Unit 2 Section A or Section B. The specification clearly states that the choice is in the hands of your teacher with as much consultation with you as the teacher feels is necessary. There is a balance between ownership, guidance and direction here that most teachers will recognise for you. My job as examiner is to assess your contribution to the performance in relation to the criteria, not to make a judgement in relation to the choice itself. Whilst there is no such thing as a 'suitable' text, there are ways to make a text 'suitable' for this examination. 'Popular' texts we may come across more than once this year are likely to include:

- *The Crucible* by Arthur Miller
- *My Mother Said I Never Should* by Charlotte Keatley
- *Animal Farm* by Peter Hall (from George Orwell)
- *Find Me* by Olwyn Wymark
- *Accidental Death of an Anarchist* by Dario Fo
- *The Trial* by Steven Berkoff
- *East Is East* by Ayub Khan-Din

Next year it might well be a combination of, amongst others:

- *Our Country's Good* by Timberlake Wertenbaker
- *The Importance of Being Earnest* by Oscar Wilde
- *Bouncers* by John Godber
- *The Government Inspector* by Nikolai Gogol
- *Road* by Jim Cartwright

There is nothing to say that you must not perform in a production of a text that we may see a number of times. If it is appropriate for another school of college, then it may be appropriate for you.

Every year we see fresh and exciting productions of old favourites, alongside productions of plays that will be new to us in this unit. It is always exciting to see new plays presented for examination performance, and it is really good to see the diversity of material on offer each year from around the world. It is the judgement of your teacher, based on his or her understanding of you as an individual and as a member of the production group, as to what will be suitable for you to perform and give you the opportunity to access the marks.

This is equally true for theatre-design candidates. In planning for this unit, you must be very clear that any member of your group who decides to choose this option has the opportunity to be involved fully in the process in order for them to be able to access the marks on an equal footing with you.

The design candidate needs to be fully involved in all aspects of the production, and it is up to your director and you to ensure that the experience is as valuable for the design candidate as it is for you.

Your design candidate is earning exactly the same amount of marks for this unit as you are, and this is equally so for both sections. They are just earning their marks in a different way and with more emphasis on written evidence.

Your examiner is looking for a contribution from a design candidate that will potentially allow them to access up to 60 per cent of the marks for the AS year if they choose to offer design in both Section A and Section B. What your teacher must consider in Section B is if there enough for them to do in order to enable them to access the marks and whether your school or college has the equipment, facilities and expertise to guide a design candidate.

13 Group performance

PREPARING FOR SECTION B

This is a different challenge and one that your teacher will be heavily involved in with you as your director. The group performance gives you the opportunity to explore character within situation and enables the visiting examiner to see your contribution to the work of the group. Section B is worth exactly the same marks as Section A and therefore needs equal attention from you with the group in mind. In this section, we are going to look at some possible ideas for performance with suggestions for how you might approach the group performance with the examiner in mind. You are all working towards individual marks (40 marks is 30 per cent of the AS year), but your contribution to the group earns you those marks.

CHOOSING THE TEXT FOR SECTION B

The choice of text for Section B is important as the decision will have an impact on your 30 per cent of the marks available for the AS year. Some factors for you and your teacher to consider are:

- the size and make-up of the group;
- the number of teachers(-directors) in relation to the number of students and the number of performance groups;
- the personal interests and strengths of the teacher(s) – whilst teachers like to be challenged by material, they will also have an eye on the assessment criteria and will look to finding a text with you that will enable you to access the marks;
- the gender of the students – although Edexcel has no issue with cross-gender casting, decisions to do this should not be taken lightly and must suit the context of the piece itself;
- the available space;

- the impact of the Unit 2 performance on other users of the space – other examination performances, for example;
- the capabilities of the group – this is a professional judgement your teacher will make with you in relation to challenge and appropriateness for this level of study;
- the requirements of the examination as set out in the specification and the updated information issued each year by the Examination Board;
- the time available to devote to the process – the Unit 2 performance in relation to Unit 1 and other school/college events and deadlines that you may not be aware of but that your teacher must take into account in the planning of the examination;
- connections with Unit 1 texts, practitioners and theatre visits; accommodating theatre-design candidates – if any;
- the complexities of the text in terms of themes and language and the implications of this on the preparation time;
- the suitability of the text for this level of study;
- the cutability of the text (will it edit successfully?);
- the enjoyment factor – challenging but not daunting.

You may not have considered some of the above but you do need to be aware that your teacher will not take decisions lightly in relation to these. Your teacher may be very open with you, while others will make decisions and then involve their students in the process of preparing for the performance. There are no rules about this, and no recommendations. Most teachers will agree, however, that the more collaborative the process is at this level of study, the more opportunities there are for students to achieve. There needs to be a balance here, though, with the ultimate responsibility for keeping the course – and you and your fellow students – on track resting with the teacher. If in doubt, you must ask. You are also balancing preparing for Section A while the process of selecting and rehearsing Section B is under way, and there will need to be some really clear stepping stones set in place very early on in the process so you, as an individual and as a member of a performance group, have a clear understanding of the time scale involved.

FACING THE CHALLENGE

The whole unit is worth 60 per cent of the AS course, and, therefore, there needs to be appropriate challenge in the choice(s) your teacher makes. A really important consideration in relation to the specification is the word *challenge*. Our opinion on this is that the challenge lies in the theatrical interpretation of the play, rather than necessarily in the play itself, and there is a need for your teacher to be as sure as possible about the capabilities of the individuals in the group before decisions are made about the choice of the Section B text and an interpretation of it that will allow you all to have access to the marks available.

Of course the decision is important: it impacts on a large percentage of your final marks. Be prepared for your teacher to change his or her mind or to try out a few extracts with you as he or she gets to know you and to work with you more during the autumn term. You may be set some of the monologue or duologue tasks from earlier in this section, for example, or similar extracts from your Unit 1 texts to explore, which not only will be beneficial to your work on Unit 1 but will also help your teacher to gain a better understanding of your capabilities across a range of potential texts.

Exploration in Unit 1 is a great strategy for experimenting with Unit 2 in mind and for letting your teacher try different combinations within your group in order to gain more of a sense of performance potential. This is just as true for Section A as it is for Section B of Unit 2.

MAKING DECISIONS FOR YOU

Your reaction to decisions your teacher will make with you on your behalf is all to do with decisions about working you need to make at this level of study. Smart students make smart decisions – and work smart for their grades. Look around the room again and consider the following in relation to those around you. It would be wrong to be judgemental about any of the statements that follow, but it is right to be aware of them – your teacher has to be.

Potential problems, possible solutions

Within the cross-section of people around you, consider that some people in the group (including you!) may struggle with the following problems:

- Complex language. This does not mean your teacher needs to avoid a text that contains complex language, but what it does mean is that he or she needs to be aware of this and to offer appropriate support to all students during the rehearsal process.
- Themes and issues in plays. The challenge of *Closer* by Patrick Marber, for example, is the ability of the group to deal with the very mature themes and language of the play – effectively used to explore these very complex and ultimately destructive relationships – from the perspective of (mainly) a group of seventeen-year-olds. Your teacher will need to balance this decision against the assessment criteria and how successfully

he or she feels individuals will be able to perform in a production of this kind of complex text.

- Being there on a regular basis for a variety of reasons. The whole process of rehearsing for Unit 2 and the commitment that is involved in creating a performance will be a challenge to some members of your group who may find attending school/college on regular basis challenging in itself. This may mean that your teacher may make the decision to present Jim Cartwright's *Two* or Duffy and Supple's *Grimm Tales* or *Arabian Nights* for example, based primarily on the need to accommodate the nature and dynamics of the group, rather than the more obvious theatrical merits of the individual pieces.

- The acting skills required. Your teacher will try to ensure that the process is supportive in recognising everyone's capabilities and incorporating their performances into the whole, rather than isolating those who struggle. Some may have difficulty in learning and delivering very long and complex monologues. This does not mean that they should be excluded from playing, for example, Liz Morden in *Our Country's Good.* There is nothing to stop somebody who may struggle with the dialogue from playing Liz as long as your teacher makes decisions in the editing of the text. The very long and challenging speech about Liz's life in London, for example, will edit well. (See pp. 112–13.) The assessment criteria cover a range of performance skills, and the examiner will take into account physical and vocal qualities in a balanced way. Your teacher will aim to develop the potential of everybody in your group, which may mean exploring strengths of individuals in the way the chosen text is edited and cast for performance.

- Being part of the group. People will have very personal and highly individual ideas about approaches to their roles and to the piece as a whole in performance. They will have opinions about everything and will try to influence the way the performance takes shape, mainly for personal benefit – but not always. The challenge for your teacher is to encourage involvement, participation and input whilst making it very clear from the outset that the director will always have the final decision about every aspect of the production and demonstrating this very firmly early on in the process.

Bearing all of this in mind, consider that the individuals around you in your drama space will make up the performance group(s) for Unit 2 Section B. Your main concern during the process of creating the Unit 2 Section B production must be to give of your best at all times in relation to what your teacher-director is trying to create with you. There will be times during the process when you will feel pressured and times during the process when you will feel neglected – most of the time you will feel like it is somewhere in

Figure 13.1
This group of nine students worked very successfully as an ensemble, mainly on the tiny stage you see here. It required discipline and good organisation.

Source: Alan Perks and Jacqueline Porteous.

between. Your teacher-director has the overview and the task of keeping you all on track, juggling time as necessary to enable everybody to access the text and the concept in order to create the production. Rehearsal is about developing and improving, preparing for performance and individual contributions to that process. It is also about having fun and rising to the challenge of the various stages you will go through. Rehearsal is also about discipline. How disciplined are you?

HOW DISCIPLINED ARE YOU?

Answer yes or no to the following ten statements:

1. I can work on my own in a room when other people are listening to music and apparently enjoying themselves.
2. I can make a decision about an item of clothing and not be influenced by the opinions of others.
3. I am able to focus on the task in hand and not be put off when other people do not appear to need to work so hard.
4. I can learn lines easily with a set routine each day in order to learn them quickly.
5. I always attend rehearsals with my script, notebook and pencil and make notes on directorial decisions regularly.
6. I can prepare a monologue on my own with little input from others.

7. I always meet deadlines and am able to multi-task effectively, prioritising by both date and importance.
8. I can say no to a night out when I know that there is work to be done.
9. I am able to strike an appropriate work–life balance depending on the demands on me at a particular time.
10. I can offer support to others without neglecting my own work.

THE TEACHER'S UNIT

For the vast majority of drama teachers, this is the unit that gets them going, the one they look forward to as it enables them to have a definite creative input into a very public aspect of the assessment process. It is also extremely challenging for your teacher because of the very public nature of the assessment.

EDITING THE TEXT

Almost any decision your teacher-director makes regarding choice of text will almost inevitably involve him or her in some editing in order to prepare it for the examination. With a minimum performance time of fifteen minutes and a maximum of sixty minutes, your teacher-director will have clear decisions to make about either choosing a one-act play within the time limits or editing a longer text to provide a suitable vehicle for your work. Whatever the options, there is a range of opinions on how much students should be involved in the process of preparing a text for performance but the focus of your attention is that the examiner will be coming to see your performance on an agreed date sometime between February and May, and, once that date has been fixed, it is extremely difficult to change it except in extreme circumstances. Not being ready may be an extreme circumstance for you and your group, but whether the Exam Board will sanction it as a reasonable reason for postponement is a different matter.

WHAT TO DO – AND HOW TO DO IT

On a very basic level, your main concern as far as your group piece is concerned is threefold:

1. Who is my character?
2. How does my character fit into the whole of this teacher-director interpretation?
3. How do I access the marks through my performance?

Your teacher-director will have very similar concerns to yours, but multiply yours by the number of people there are in your group, and this will give you an idea of the challenge your teacher faces in this unit. Your contribution to the whole process will be largely dictated by your teacher's approach to rehearsal, with you responding positively by learning your lines as soon as possible and preparing for scenes in advance so you are not stumbling over the basics in a rehearsal that is trying to move you on. You could also be considerate of others and supportive of those who may be struggling with, for example, learning lines or responding to specifics of direction. If you get what your director is looking for, there is nothing to stop you helping others to understand it too. The role of the critical friend becomes vital during this process.

CREATING THE GROUPS: WHO GOES WHERE, AND WHY?

The combination of students is very important for your teacher-director to consider. The best way for us to look at it is to consider again an imaginary group of twelve acting students. For the purpose of this example, we will be looking at two performances, each lasting around twenty-five to thirty minutes, with combinations of five and seven students or six and six students in each. This could very well be your group, so think of those people around you in your lessons as you look at the possible permutations your teacher may want to consider with you when coming to a decision about who goes where – and why.

If we were to split our imaginary group into an eight and a four, however, there would be a very strong case for looking at a performance nearer twenty minutes than forty minutes for the group of four and keeping close to the forty-minute time limit for the group of eight. There is a notional idea of approximately five minutes per person in the group but, clearly there is some variation in this if the maximum group size of nine allows for a performance time of a maximum of sixty minutes.

The idea is that we give you as performer enough acting time to demonstrate to the examiner your performance skills within the piece – but not so much time that you then start to lose your way. You would be surprised at how easy it is for a performance candidate to 'lose the way'. A simple moment of distraction towards the end of the performance may be enough to influence your examiner on the awarding of marks, and it is really important to remain focused throughout the performance at all times – even if you think you are not the centre of attention at that particular time in the piece. Assume that the examiner is looking at you all of the time.

Another tip to avoid losing the way – and the opportunity to access marks – is not to look to see if the examiner is looking at you. There is almost an

Figure 13.2

This group is rehearsing to a younger class to gauge audience feedback. Note that the examiner's desk is already there so that the actors grow accustomed to it.

Source: Alan Perks and Jacqueline Porteous.

inevitability in the fact that when you look at examiners to see if they are looking at you – they will be!

CHOICE OF TEXT LEADS TO SUCCESS

There is no doubt that where Unit 2 Section B is less successful in larger centres, it tends to be because the choice of texts has left students floundering with difficult and complex characterisations within pieces they have struggled to understand, and, because teacher-directors are juggling more than one piece, each has not been given the attention the unit deserves. This tends to be more in centres where there are two or three performance groups, rather than six of seven groups – for obvious reasons. Centres with six or seven performance groups tend to have more than one member of staff teaching the course in a number of teaching groups, and, therefore, Unit 2 directing is divided between a number of different teachers. Clearly your teacher is under pressure whether there are twelve of you on the course or 112, but there are ways of managing groups that will hopefully help to limit the pressure. Your teacher may decide to prepare more than one version of the same text with you – there is nothing in the examination rubric to say that this should not be done.

EXAMPLE: *OH! WHAT A LOVELY WAR* BY JOAN LITTLEWOOD

This is an **episodic** piece that explores the absurdities and tragedies of the First World War with 'some songs, some battles and a few jokes'. If you are in a teaching group of twelve, then your teacher may cut the original script in two different ways, each for six actors, creating two versions of the same text in which some episodes may be the same but a lot will be different. Your teacher-director may then have a different interpretation in mind for each version in order to differentiate them enough for the examiner but not so much that the point of the exercise is lost. One version may focus on the Home Front while the other may focus on the Trenches, but the two versions together will define the original for the audience and, of course, for your examiner. This same text will edit equally as well for three groups of six or seven students as there are enough 'episodes' within it to allow some overlap but a lot of originality between two or three different versions of it.

Whatever the circumstances, experience tells us that candidates tend to be more able to sustain their performances in pieces towards the lower end of the recommended time limits than those towards the top end.

The whole of Section B depends on your teacher-director making the right choice for you as an individual and for your group as a whole. As well as considering the group, your teacher may also have an eye on Section A texts in order to either complement or contrast – or both, for you and your examiner – in relation to the Section B experience.

Experience tells us that episodic pieces are easier to edit for this unit than plays with a 'more traditional' structure. This is not to say that your teacher should not choose *The Importance of Being Earnest, The Government Inspector, A Doll's House* or *An Inspector Calls* because they have a more 'traditional' structure and therefore may not be considered suitable texts for Unit 2 Section B. There are different – and at times more complex – editing skills needed with this type of play in order to make the final version a coherent whole for the purposes of the examination.

The key to all of this is to remember that the text is being prepared for an examination performance and choices made with this in mind may not be the same choices made under other circumstances. The text is your vehicle to enable you to access your marks, and there are texts that appear to be more appropriate for this than others. Again, as with all things, we are very much aware that there are always exceptions to rules.

The episodic nature of *Our Country's Good,* for example, lends itself to the Unit 2 Section B approach very well. The play was written to be multi-roled, and there is no sense of gender biases in the script, with cross-gender casting of most of the roles – particularly convicts to officers – quite common. There are a number of themes in the play and a number of ways that it may

episodic

A play written in short scenes or episodes that help create an almost cinematic feel for the performance and encourages a fast-paced production.

be edited for performance in order to highlight one or more of the chosen themes. Most plays by Brecht offer similar possibilities, and their structure allows for them to be edited and reshaped in imaginative ways for the requirements of this unit with performance opportunities clearly defined.

POSSIBLE TEXTS FOR UNIT 2, SECTION B

The following is not an exhaustive list but represents a range of texts, interpretations of which have featured regularly as examination performances.

* Albee, Edward (1962) *Who's Afraid of Virginia Woolf?*
* Anouilh, Jean (1944) *Antigone.*
* Aron, Geraldine (1991) *The Donahue Sisters.*
* Bond, Edward (1985) *The Tin Can People.*
* Brecht, Bertolt (1928) *The Threepenny Opera.*
* Brecht, Bertolt (1941) *The Resistible Rise of Arturo Ui.*
* Brecht, Bertolt (1943) *The Good Person of Szechwan.*
* Campton, David (1976) *The Cagebirds.*
* Cartwright, Jim (1991) *Bed.*
* Churchill, Caryl (1982) *Top Girls.*
* Churchill, Caryl (1994) *The Skriker.*
* Cooke, Dominic (1998) *Arabian Nights.*
* Daniels, Sarah (1988) *The Gut Girls.*
* Delaney, Shelagh (1958) *A Taste of Honey.*
* Duffy, Carol Ann, dramatised by Tim Supple (1996) *Grimm Tales.*
* Fo, Dario (1970) *Accidental Death of an Anarchist.*
* Fo, Dario (1974) *Can't Pay? Won't Pay!*
* Friel, Brian (1985) *Lovers.*
* Friel, Brian (1990) *Dancing at Lughnasa.*
* Godber, John (1983) *Bouncers.*
* Godber, John (1985) *Shakers.*
* Godber, John (1987) *Teechers.*
* Karge, Manfred (1988) *The Conquest of the South Pole.*
* Lavery, Bryony (1997) *More Light.*
* Lochhead, Liz (1989) *Dracula.*
* Lochhead, Liz (1997) *Cuba.*
* Lochhead, Liz (2003) *Thebans.*
* Lorca, Federico García (1936) *The House of Bernarda Alba.*
* Marowitz, Charles (1968) *Hamlet.*
* Miller, Arthur (1953) *The Crucible.*
* Miller, Arthur (1955) *A View from the Bridge.*
* Orton, Joe (1965) *Loot.*

- Owen, Bill (1973) *The Laundry Girls.*
- Shaffer, Peter (1973) *Equus.*
- Shakespeare, William (1594–6?) *A Midsummer Night's Dream.*
- Shakespeare, William (1610–11) *The Tempest.*
- Stoppard, Tom (1962) *The Real Inspector Hound.*
- Thomas, Dylan (1954) *Under Milk Wood.*
- Wheeler, Mark (1999) *Too Much Punch for Judy.*
- Whelan, Peter (1984) *The Accrington Pals.*
- Wymark, Olwyn (1980) *Find Me.*

How many of the plays on the list do you:

1. know well?
2. do you know?
3. have heard of?
4. have never heard of?

Extension Activity

Exploring texts

Compile a list of three or four of the plays on our list and set yourself the target of reading them over the course of three or four weeks – you can always come back for more.

Some of the texts on the list could provide examples of possible monologues and duologues for Unit 2, Section A so it might be worth exploring these texts first, particularly if you are looking at the Section A monologues and duologues as potential examination pieces. By reading some of the texts on our list, you will get a flavour of how different playwrights operating in different genre and time periods structure their plays and the depth of information they give to the reader and the potential actor/director of the piece.

The decision about your Section B text is in the hands of your teacher-director and should not be made based solely on this list alone – it is not exhaustive, nor is it exclusive. The list represents a range of playwrights and a range of plays, some of which are mentioned at other stages in this book, others of which are new to this list. There are, for example, other play texts mentioned elsewhere in this book, and nothing should replace the professional judgement of your teacher based on his or her understanding of you and your group and your capabilities in relation to this unit. Budgets may be tight, but the Drama Department will have been given an allocation of funding to support the teaching of this course, so there should not be any concern about affordability of texts. Some schools and colleges charge students for copies of texts, which means that you will have your own copy afterwards – not a bad thing really, and it does mean that you can annotate your own copy as much as you like once you have paid for it.

The Examiner says:

For this examination there is no list of recommended plays, just as there is no list of unsuitable plays. It is up to your teacher to decide the text(s), and it is the performance of the text that I am interested in. Teachers will often ask for a recommended text that will be suitable for their students. What they are really looking for is a text that has earned other students high marks in the examination, with the assumption being that it will do the same for their students. That, of course, is impossible to predict. I do not have access to you on a daily basis, so I have no idea how your group functions in exploring practical drama. It would therefore be very wrong for me to recommend anything to you for performance. What the lists in this book do is give an indication of what others have used successfully for examination performance. The final choice is with you and your teacher.

On the day of the examination, your individual contribution will earn you your marks, so you need to ensure that you are visibly engaged throughout the performance in order to convince me against the published criteria – in both Section A and Section B, actor or designer.

My normal approach to awarding marks is to watch your performance within the piece and to make notes during the performance against the criteria. I am not making notes about you in relation to other performers, but in relation to the criteria – and my understanding of the national standard for this unit.

Having said that, it is sometimes useful to me to put you and your group into rank order, from the highest mark to the lowest against the criteria. At this stage, I am looking at the band I think your performance will put you in, not necessarily the mark you should have within that band. It is only later after a period of thinking time that I will go away and award you a specific mark against each of the assessment criteria, giving you a total mark for your performance. If you are offering a design skill for either section, then the process is almost identical. I will take into account the information you give me during your presentation and your written rationale and will then look at how your ideas are realised within the performance and how they integrate with the overall concept/interpretation of the piece. It is the realisation in performance that is key, and any judgement of marks will be based on the reality of the design and how successfully it has been integrated into the whole. No decision on marks is made on the day of the examination.

There is, therefore, no point in asking your teacher what I thought of your performance or design and what mark you might have been given. Your teacher will not know – because I will not know. As your examiner, my job is to be as objective as I possibly can and to award you as many marks as I possibly can against the criteria. I have absolutely no opinion about the choice of text, the casting of roles or the interpretation your teacher-director will bring to the piece. Yours may be the fifth *Road* I have seen in a week or the third *Caucasian Chalk Circle;* it does not matter. My judgement is about your performance in your production of the piece. You may perform in full costume under full stage lights within elaborate settings – or you may present your piece in your drama studio with a basic design concept. I have no opinion about these decisions in relation to the assessment criteria – unless, of course, you have a design candidate in your group responsible for lighting, in which case I need to be able to identify that contribution in relation to the lighting of the piece.

As a drama practitioner, I will have an opinion about a whole range of plays, playwrights, styles and genres. As an examiner I have a specific focus to my work with you, and that is to award you as many marks as I possibly can against the published criteria for this unit.

Figure 13.3
This is the view taken from the examiner's desk. The examiner should have the best view in the house so that he or she can pick up every gesture and detail, no matter how small.

CASTING

The final decision as to casting must rest with your teacher-director. He or she may hold auditions or may be more dictatorial. A lot will depend on the make-up of the group – and on the piece itself, of course. Your director will choose particular texts for this unit because he or she can see particular students performing specific roles, and, if this is the case, the other members of the group will often fall into place in the planning. In special circumstances, there may a text that will suit all members of your group, but this is highly unlikely.

The main considerations in casting are:

- the individuals in the group and what you can bring to the piece;
- the assessment criteria and how you can demonstrate accessing the skills;
- vocal and physical considerations in relation to individual roles;
- the potential for creativity, and the potential for clashes;
- the overall look and feel of the piece in performance.

Your teacher as director will have ideas for casting in mind, probably developing these as you go through Unit 1. Initial casting may not be in tablets of stone, and there may be some leeway during the process, but everything that is finalised to do with this performance must be finalised by your teacher-director.

THE PROCESS FOR SECTION B

Outline rehearsal schedule: *Two* by Jim Cartwright

Table 13.1 *Outline rehearsal schedule*

Week	Section	Activity	Homework	Success indicator
1	Whole play	Read through	Re-read	All know the play
2	Pair work – first half	Work in pairs in the first half with each actor playing two roles	Write up activity – analyse contrast in two roles played	Understanding of the relationships within pairs in the first half
3	Pair work – second half	Work in pairs in the second half with each actor playing two roles	Write up activity – analyse contrast in all roles played so far	Understanding of the structure of the play as a whole
4	Explore the monologues	Work on the individual roles in the play from the list	Prepare a speech from one of your monologues to present to the group	Each of you has a monologue to present to the group
5	Casting decisions	Exploring possible combinations	Read the play again with your roles in mind	Initial casting complete – everybody happy
6	Blocking week	Exploring the stage space with audience in mind	Read the play again with blocking in mind	Blocking complete

It is probably good practice (and sets a clear example for your preparation for Unit 3 in the A2 year) if the rehearsal process is as formal as possible with a clear schedule drawn up as early on in the process as possible so everybody understands the proposed time scale and the milestones along the way. The outline schedule here demonstrates six weeks from a rehearsal period, the first three weeks of which will be planned in detail in advance and then reviewed before the second block of three weeks is planned. Your director will let you know the proposed week of the examination performance as soon as possible: this will avoid any potential clashes with other subjects or outside interests. The proposed week and day of examination is subject to confirmation by the Examination Board but for the vast majority of examinations the examiner is usually able to accommodate first- or second-choice dates. When you have the proposed week in your diary, therefore, it is probably safe to assume that the exam performance will take place during that week – unless there are particular unforeseen circumstances that may change the arrangements. Your Section A monologue, duologue or design realisation needs to be ready at the same time, particularly if you are in a centre with a smaller number of candidates, so there is plenty for you to be getting on with in the spring term. Even if you are in a centre with a large number of candidates and the examiner will be visiting more than once, there is a stated period in which this examination must take place so you need to be working within that. It is amazing how quickly time goes when you are busy and deadlines are looming. It is likely that Section A will go first in a typical examination session, and, should you be in a centre that has more than one examiner visit, then this is still likely to be the case.

GET-IT-RIGHT PRODUCTIONS PRESENTS . . .

Some students and their teacher-director form a theatre company to present Unit 2, and this gives the whole process an essential air of importance and formality (see the information sheet on p. 143), and it also gives a discipline to the process, particularly when there are so many other demands on your time as well. We all have different ways of working, and the specification encourages this. What is not subject to negotiation or change or to personal taste and experience, however, is the standard of the examination, and it must be remembered throughout the process – and, indeed, the specification – that your work is always seen in relation to other students across the country, not in relation to those people sitting around you in the room at this moment, however much you may value their opinions. It is probably a good idea to have another look around you at this point and to decide who are the performers you rate in the room. What is it about their performance skills that really impresses you within the group – and what can you learn from them in order to improve your own performance? This is a delicate process because sometimes we spend so much time looking at the qualities of others that we neglect to develop our own qualities when the reality often is that we have exactly the same potential as those who we look up to, we just do not actively encourage ourselves towards our own goals because we are too busy being in awe of others.

You may find, therefore, that the people you admire the most may not have qualities so very different from your own but they may have a more confident way of presenting themselves that makes it look as though they are better, more confident performers. You may also find that there are people who look to you for your performance skills in the same way as you look to others. You are all different, and you all contribute to the totality of a performance in different ways – and this is something that your teacher will try to recognise in compiling the performance groups for Unit 2. Your teacher will provide the outside eye – a necessary quality when directing work as it has a more objective overview than those people who are caught up in the middle of the performance – i.e. you.

Extension Activity

Exploring the actor's craft

- Make a list of your top five actors.
- Alongside each name, say why you admire their work and give examples of roles you have seen them in that have particularly impressed you.
- What performance skills did they use in these roles in order to engage you?
- How did they adapt the skills to the roles?

INFORMATION SHEET FOR UNIT 2 SECTION B

Forming a production company: Get-it-Right Productions

A major advantage of forming a production company to prepare for Unit 2 is that it puts you in the driving seat and helps you to structure your work in relation to the time scale of the rehearsal process and the demands placed upon you by other subject areas.

It is probably a good idea to talk with your teacher-director about this at the end of the autumn term just when you are starting to think about the demands of Unit 2 and how they are going to impact upon you in the time set aside for rehearsal.

The main thing you need to know at the start of the rehearsal process is the date of the examination performance(s). Your teacher-director will have a date in mind, subject to confirmation by the Examination Board. Once this date has been confirmed, then this must be the date you are working towards.

The idea behind setting up the company is to enable you to access your teacher-director and to 'buy-in' his or her time to direct particular scenes or sections of the text in a structured pattern and to monitor the overall production as it emerges. This is particularly important if you have one teacher-director working with more than one production group. The very first session should plan the rehearsal outline for the weeks ahead, very clearly structuring the process so that all of your company will know the focus of each rehearsal and prepare accordingly and, once the structure has been agreed/formulated with your teacher-director, it is important to stick to it with the proviso that it may be reviewed at regular intervals during the process. Your teacher-director will certainly have a major input into the planning here as he or she will have a rehearsal schedule in mind early on in the process, and it is worth remembering this when the outline pattern is compiled. A major advantage of being this organised is that it means unforeseen circumstances that may take your teacher-director away from the group are covered in that you will still be able to rehearse.

Rehearsal schedule

Once the pattern has been agreed and noted by everybody, each session/ rehearsal should start and end with a five-minute company meeting to remind and refresh ideas ready for the session ahead. There is a real discipline involved in making sure these five-minute slots are preserved but, in the long run, it is really important to recognise the importance of forward planning and review of progress in relation to the performance dates. The rehearsal process is not just about preparing the individual roles within the piece but it is also about the overall concept for the production, and this may involve you and your company in additional tasks around technical aspects of the production. The overall feel of being in a company should not be neglected, but the main emphasis must be on making sure that you have access to the marks available for this unit.

The teacher-director

Whilst the approach to creating Unit 2 Section B is collaborative, there are clear decision-making moments from the teacher-director that move the process on towards the performance and keep you on track during the rehearsals in order to make sure that you are ready on performance day. Your teacher-director must keep the momentum going, and you must all have an eye on the deadlines if you are going to be able to give of your best for your examiner.

Within the process of creating the performance for this unit there is really no time to be sidetracked into too much introspective examination of the playwright's art, and, really, there is no demand for this in any aspect of the exam, other than to support your approach to Unit 2, which builds on the techniques for exploration you have used in Unit 1 and ideas you have been introduced to as part of a structured induction period. You will need to create a rationale for Section A in which you need to demonstrate something of your understanding of the playwright's work, and this process will help with your overall understanding of your Section B play.

Your teacher may look at creating a **pre-life** sequence, for example, as a legitimate part of a rehearsal for Section B. This could be seen as very

pre-life
A Stanislavskian technique of looking at what was going on in the life of a character before the events of the play, used to help an actor gain a greater understanding of why a character may react in a particular way in the life of the play.

simplistic in that it involves reading and understanding the text but arguably no real in-depth research. For both sections of Unit 2, however, this kind of activity could help you to explore character and relationships, which, in turn, could help in your final performance. Whilst there is no requirement for in-depth research, there may be specific rehearsal techniques which can be used to enhance and develop your understanding of your part within the piece as a whole and which your teacher needs to introduce at regular intervals – or as appropriate – during the rehearsals.

The purpose of exploring rehearsal techniques as part of preparing for Section B therefore is not necessarily to reinforce Stanislavsky, for example, as a rehearsal practitioner at this stage but to gain an understanding of your current level of understanding of the play and its historical, social or cultural context for the purposes of the rehearsal in order for you to continue to develop your role(s) in relation to your teacher's interpretation.

The relationship between characters must be made clear to you, and the opportunity to start to map some of those relationships early on in the rehearsal process is a useful one. Your teacher-director will have an eye on the bigger picture of the production and will employ a number of approaches in order for you to be able to contribute positively to that whole.

MAKING CONNECTIONS ACROSS THE UNITS

Think holistically: remember what has gone before and what is to come and structure your response to Unit 2 accordingly. It is sometimes the case that students will see this Unit 2 experience in isolation, rather than connecting it back into Unit 1 and, indeed, into their GCSE as appropriate. There is an awful lot of experience to be drawn upon here, and your teacher may or may not make this connection explicit for you. This unit is about performance and draws together all of your experiences to date, including those around exploring a text and your experience as a member of an audience, presuming that you have been part of an audience by this stage in the course. You may not have formally been to the theatre as a group by the time you start work on Unit 2, depending on the time scale you are working on and how your teacher chooses to approach Unit 1 with you. You may, however, have been on a theatre visit socially or with another department – if you are studying English, for example – and this experience is always relevant to your understanding of how theatre works in performance.

This unit is also about looking forward to the A2 year when you will be much more in control of your performance work in relation to Unit 3 and in the role of director in preparing for Unit 4, the written unit. Everything that happens here should also inform what happens in the A2 year.

REHEARSAL TECHNIQUES

The following are some of the more popular rehearsal techniques used by teacher-directors in preparing for Unit 2 Section B. You may have come across some of them, possibly in exploring in Unit 1. We explain and explore these techniques and others in more detail on the website that accompanies this book. Your teacher-director may use a range of other techniques too, and there is nothing hard and fast about any of this: a lot of it is down to personal choice.

Rehearsal techniques could include:

- actioning key words;
- emotional memory;
- exploring status;
- hot-seating;
- magic if;
- pre-life;
- off-text work;
- tableaux;
- thought-tracking;
- units and objectives;
- writing in role;
- character on the wall.

Work progressed by Stanislavsky features heavily in this list – and rightly so – but as we mentioned earlier in this chapter, there are other practitioners whose work may well inspire rehearsal workshops and give opportunities for you to develop your understanding of creating performance, based also on your experience of exploring texts and practitioners for Unit 1.

Extension Activity

Rehearsal techniques

Choose three of the rehearsal techniques from the list and prepare a section of script with these techniques in mind to show how and why they could be useful in preparing for performance. The section should ideally be a complete scene, and your three techniques could be demonstrated in a workshop lasting approximately twenty minutes with your group. For further explanation of rehearsal techniques, see the website that accompanies this book.

THE PURPOSE OF THE REHEARSAL

The purpose of rehearsal is to improve, to gain a greater understanding of the character(s) within the piece in relation to the director and the play-wright's original intentions. There are a number of approaches to rehearsing for performance, all of which recognise that the final interpretation of individual characters contributes to the audience's overall understanding of the production. The purpose of rehearsal is very straightforward and should be really obvious but it is worth thinking about rehearsals in relation to the tasks to be undertaken for Unit 2. Rehearsals allow for experimentation and exploration and give you the opportunity to ask the question 'What if?' and the freedom to explore within that. For example:

* What if my character has a cockney accent?
* What if my character walks with a limp?
* What if my character fiddles nervously with a scarf, a handbag or a handkerchief?
* What if my character wears a hat, jacket, overcoat, hooded top or scarf?
* What if my character holds a cup, glass, packet of mints or a piece of fruit?

It is equally valid to apply the 'what if' principle if you are a design candidate. The above statements can be modified very simply to accommodate costume design, for example. For technical aspects of design, again, the principle is the same: the scope of the questions will just be broader to accommodate the demands of, say, the lighting plot.

A STRUCTURED APPROACH TO CHARACTER: EXPLORE AND PERFECT

Explore

Look at the obvious and not-so-obvious approaches to the character and find ways of getting under their skin in order to present your version in a way that engages your audience in a very short period of time. In looking at exploring, it is worth referencing work undertaken for Unit 1 of the specification as there may be ideas within that unit that will help you with this one.
Ways of exploring could include:

* in-role writing
* actioning text
* role reversal/swap

- hot-seating
- conscience alley.

Perfect

Create and fine-tune the nuances of the role to the point where you feel as though you inhabit the character physically and vocally within the confines of the chosen performance space. Ways of perfecting could include:

- physical exploration in relation to props and costume;
- connect micro- and macro-movements to specific lines;
- apply vocal nuances to specific words/lines;
- speed running of sections;
- exploring proxemics with audience in mind.

Draw on your experiences to date. Do not forget what has gone before. For the vast majority of you, Section A preparation will run alongside Section B preparation in which you will be working with your teacher as director, an experience which will inform your own approach to Section A. Your teacher will also not leave you entirely on your own for Section A. A lot will depend on numbers and time – always time – but your teacher is well aware of the importance of Section A and will spend the appropriate amount of time with you in order to ensure that you are able to explore and perfect.

READING AND ACTIONING THE TEXT

This is really practical and an important part of preparing any script for performance. You cannot action – bring the script to life – without reading, and you need to read in order to gain something of an understanding of the playwright's intentions. It is not possible to see all the potential there is in a script simply by reading it: you can get a fair idea, but it is only when you start to create the three-dimensional version that you start to have a more rounded vision of how the characters interlock within the structure of the piece as presented on the page.

Whether you are looking at support for Section A or Section B, this is the kind of activity you could be involved in away from lesson or rehearsal time that will help you to access your role(s) more effectively and more quickly during the more formal rehearsals. Using the technique of reading and actioning alongside Stanislavsky's units and objectives could be a really useful way to help you to access your role(s). It is always important to remember that you are not working alone on this course, and the people with you can provide you with the best support if you involve them enough.

DRAMABILITY AND THE CRITICAL FRIEND

There really should be a word like *dramability* – the ability to take part in and respond to drama. As it is, we have made it up for the purposes of this section, but, you never know, it may catch on. A lot of what we have covered so far in this book has been about the holistic nature of the course and ideas for accessing the demands of Units 1 and 2 in order to achieve the best possible grade. In the introduction we talked about you and what the course would hold for you as it unfolded. This next section is about you and your 'dramability'.

How are you fitting in to the pattern of the course and what are you discovering about yourself? We suggest you tackle the following questions at regular intervals throughout the AS year and use them as a form of personal self-assessment to help you with your own target setting as you go along. It might be a good idea to look at this section once every half term, starting in October just after your first break. This exercise is only useful if you are honest with yourself – and only you will know how honest you are being!

Think realistically but be prepared to be challenged.

Consider the following ten statements and note those you consider describe you best at this time. You may pick as many statements as you like – but try to be realistic.

Dramability test, Part I

1. I am nervous about standing up in front of others to perform.
2. I find the physical aspects of performing a challenge.
3. When projecting my voice I tend to shout and lose the meaning of the words.
4. I am more confident in small groups than I am on my own.
5. I like the challenge of exploring characters from outside my own experience.
6. I consider myself to be a good actor.
7. I know little or nothing about design for the theatre.
8. I consider myself to be creative.
9. I struggle with the complex language in plays at times.
10. I often have ideas about shaping performance and express these strongly.

Now consider the following statements and note those that you think best apply to a friend in your group. Do not talk to your friend about your list at this stage or tell him or her that you are looking at the list in relation to them.

Dramability test, Part II

1. I think they are nervous about standing up in front of others to perform.
2. I think they find the physical aspects of performing a challenge.
3. When projecting their voice I think they tend to shout and lose the meaning of the words.
4. I think they are more confident in small groups than on their own.
5. I think they like the challenge of exploring characters from outside their own experience.
6. I think they consider themselves to be a good actor.
7. I think they know little or nothing about design for the theatre.
8. I think they consider themselves to be creative.
9. I think they struggle with the complex language in plays at times.
10. I think they often have ideas about shaping performance and express these strongly.

It would be interesting for you to share your list with your friend in order for them to be able to compare it with their own perception of themselves in relation to the subject at this stage. Look at this as a discussion opportunity: be prepared to justify your thoughts about your friend and to give clear examples in support of what you are thinking. It is an ongoing process, so you may also offer some thoughts on how your friend could develop – and hope that somebody will do the same for you!

You may share your thoughts anonymously, but it is probably much better to be open about it: the purpose of the activity is to explore the reality in relation to the perception, which is why there is no point in you being flattering or your friend being either too self-effacing or too arrogant at this stage.

The critical friend

A more formal way of exploring this activity would be for your teacher to 'buddy' you up at the start of the course in pairs with somebody who will become your 'critical friend' for the duration of the course. There may be an element of choice in this or your teacher may just pair you up. Either way, your 'critical friend' may be a very useful member of your group across the AS year and in supporting you through the performance elements particularly.

There are further details about being a critical friend below, but this person does not replace your normal friendship groups nor will he or she be expected to be available to you outside the confines of the lesson – although a lot of critical friends are also friends. It is not about that, however: it is about having somebody there that you can ask a question of and know you will get an honest answer.

The buddy/critical-friend system is a way of having somebody in the group who you can turn to and ask opinions from at regular intervals throughout the course. It is probably not a good idea for your critical friend/buddy to be a best friend outside the lesson as, quite often, you will tell each other what you want to hear, rather than tell each other what you need to do in order to develop the work successfully.

Your teacher will probably ask you to nominate two people in the group who you would like to be your buddy/critical friend and then your teacher will match everybody as far as possible with one person of their choice.

Even if your teacher does not formally adopt this system with your group, there is nothing to stop you informally pairing up with somebody in the group if you think it may be helpful to your work and your eventual grade. Clearly this is not replacing your teacher, who has the overview and the skills to engage you all in the elements of the course, but it does give you another person who you can ask, 'What do you think?' This could be an opportunity for you to have another member of your group to bounce ideas off before you commit yourself to them for a wider audience, and it is really useful to think of your critical friend as a sounding board – but also be prepared for an honest response; otherwise, it is pointless to ask opinions or share ideas.

ESSENTIALS OF A GROUP PERFORMANCE: THE TOP TEN

1. Do I understand what the play is about?
2. Do I understand my role(s) within my director's interpretation?
3. Am I able to demonstrate my abilities in relation to the role(s)?
4. Are there key scenes/moments for my character(s) that need a particular approach?
5. Are there complex speeches that I need to work on?
6. Are there opportunities for micro- and macro-movements within the performance for my character(s)?
7. What is my relationship with other members of the group?
8. What is my character's relationship to other characters?
9. What do I have to do to earn the marks?
10. Are there skills from elsewhere in the course that I can draw on?

The Examiner says:

Your visiting examiner will arrive with a full set of assessment descriptors, and your written performance concept or written design concept (maximum of 500 words) for Section A, and your written design concept (maximum 500 words) for Section B if you are a design-skill candidate.

The day of the performance is, of course, vitally important, but you must also be aware of the timeline in relation to that, and it is equally important that you respect the deadlines given to you by your teacher.

I need the information from you and your teacher in order for me to be able to prepare for my visit and to give me an opportunity to read the information that will help me to focus on your performance. I also have up to 10 marks to award you for your 500-word (maximum) concepts, so it is important that you recognise their value in relation to all of the other assessment areas of this unit, all of which carry equal marks.

You need to look at this carefully and choose a style for your notes that suits you best – or follow the advice given to you by your teacher on this. It is the first contact between you and your examiner, and it is important that you make a suitable impression. Presentation is important and leads your examiner into the content with a degree of confidence that you have prepared the notes from a position of knowledge and with an appropriate degree of respect for the process itself and its purpose. I will be looking for understanding reflected in your notes, and I will be looking for drama words and phrases used – and spelt – correctly. These notes have a purpose, and you need to be preparing for them alongside preparing for your performance/presentation. You only have 500 words maximum, including any annotation on your script extract, so I will be looking at how effectively you have used those words to present your ideas to me. The examples presented in this section are just that, of course, and you may find other more appropriate ways of presenting your notes. Do not forget that quality of written communication is important in all of your written work presented for assessment – including your rationale or concept.

The performance of your work or the realisation of your designs will, of course, have a major impact on your overall mark for this unit, and you should not become so wrapped up in the written process that you forget the practical realisation of your skill. This is a practical unit, and your performance work is recognised in the assessment structure.

The following two extension activities are concerned with exploring the language of character and are aimed at Unit 2, but you may also find them useful for Unit 1. They are not definitive, and your teacher may have variations on these exercises with which you are familiar. The intention here is not to burden you with more work but to have you think around the specification a little more, in the same way as the activities throughout the work book have encouraged you to do.

You may find that these exercises do not stretch you enough – in which case offer your own variations on them, and we will be pleased to hear from you.

Extension Activity

Exploring language of character I

- **Time**: thirty minutes.
- **Resources**: notebook, pen or pencil, the extract.
- **Purpose**: to explore annotation and to look at alternative ways of delivering well-known texts.

Consider the following few lines of dialogue that come from the opening of Shakespeare's *Macbeth*:

> When shall we three meet again?
> In thunder, lightning or in rain?
> When the hurlyburly's done,
> When the battle's lost and won.
> That will be ere the set of sun.
> Where the place?
> Upon the heath.
> There to meet with Macbeth.
> I come Grymalkin,
> Paddock calls.

> Anon!
> Fair is foul and foul is fair:
> Hover through the fog and filthy air.

1. Five minutes

Read the extract twice in your head then read it aloud. Jot down in your notebook the general meaning of the extract, recognising that there are three characters in the original that we have run together as one for the purposes of this activity.

2. Five minutes

Look at the first line: 'When shall we three meet again?' Break it down and try placing your emphasis on the following words in turn:

- When
- shall
- we
- three
- meet
- again.

Say the line aloud with the emphasis on each word in turn:

- *When* shall we three meet again?
- When *shall* we three meet again?
- When shall *we* three meet again? And so on.

3. Fifteen minutes

Continue the process across all the lines, choosing one word only in each line to emphasise.

4. Five minutes

Rehearse your version of the speech with your chosen emphasis in place. Share this with a partner and look for a response from your partner as to the effectiveness of the interpretation. It may sound too forced, too unnatural, too stilted or too sing-song for your tastes, but what the exercise will do is give you some understanding of the way in which a speech may be broken down and developed just by placing emphasis on different words.

It is important in this kind of activity that you are honest with each other. At this stage in your course you should be able to offer critical evaluation without your partner being offended or without you having to say 'no offence but . . .' The purpose of the exercise is to look at improvement, and any evaluation you can give each other is always welcome – and should be welcomed.

Extension Activity

Exploring language of character II

- **Time**: thirty minutes.
- **Resources**: pen or pencil, notebook.
- **Purpose**: to explore delivery in relation to content and audience.

1. Five minutes

In your notebook, jot down the words of a well-known nursery rhyme. If you are struggling with this, use 'Jack and Jill':

> Jack and Jill went up the hill,
> To fetch a pail of water.
> Jack fell down and broke his crown,
> And Jill went tumbling after.
>
> Up got Jack, and home did trot,
> As fast as he could caper.
> He went to bed and bound his head,
> With vinegar and brown paper.

2. Five minutes

Imagine you are a news reporter for one of the major bulletins and you have to introduce breaking news about the incident in your nursery rhyme. Prepare a short bulletin that contains all the necessary facts to be delivered to camera.

3. Five minutes

Deliver your report to camera (or to a friend), using appropriate tone and inflection.

4. Five minutes

Retain the essential elements of your news report but imagine you are now delivering it on *Newsround* to a much younger audience. Rehearse your report accordingly.

5. Five minutes

Deliver your report to camera (or to a friend) using appropriate tone and inflection.

6. Five minutes

Write down your thoughts about your delivery and how you think you changed it in relation to the material and the audience.

14 Section A and B: designers

Now that we have looked at the overview of Unit 2 and you have made your decision to be a theatre-design candidate, we need to look at more specific information about how you can access the marks in this unit against the assessment criteria. A lot of the general information for performance candidates will also be relevant for you, so it might be worth reading the section before this one too. This part of our Unit 2 information is much more succinct than that for performers. The design option is worth exactly the same marks as the performing option, and our brevity here is not meant to imply otherwise.

This unit could be about you:

- contributing to a group performance for Section B;
- contributing to a monologue or a duologue for Section A;
- experiencing the process of rehearsal and shaping the outcome through your design input;
- making interpretative decisions in relation to the text and the interpretation or concept;
- experiencing your theatre-design input impacting upon an audience.

Your teacher-director will lead you through the process of developing your chosen design skill in relation to the Section B group performance and will guide you towards your contribution to the monologue or duologue for Section A with examination conditions in mind.

The Edexcel specification clearly sets out the requirements for this unit and tells us the following:

Texts should be chosen that offer students the opportunity to exhibit their acting or design skills that are the essential object of assessment. Centres should consider the skills, experience, and prior learning of candidates in choosing texts that will engage candidates' interest throughout the considerable preparation and rehearsal time needed for this unit.

The visiting examiner will assess your contribution to performance and award you a criteria-based mark out of 80 (40 for each section, 10 marks for each element). The purpose of the preparation you will be involved in for this unit is to enable you to access the marks, in the same way as performance candidates will access the marks for their piece as performed to the examiner that will be developed from a structured rehearsal process. The approach you adopt to the process will not only inform your presentation but will also help you to access your marks for the concept.

As a theatre-design candidate, you need to consider carefully your options here, not only in relation to selecting the skill you are going to offer but also whether or not you wish to offer design for both sections of this unit. There is absolutely no pressure on you to offer design for Section B if you have decided to do so for Section A. Your decision needs to be taken in relation to the facilities and equipment you have access to and, probably more importantly, what you and your teacher think you will be able to achieve in relation to the assessment criteria and the marks you hope to earn. Your teacher will explain the requirements and the options in more detail, but it is worth noting that the design option in both Section A and Section B requires a great deal of written and diagrammatical support in order to indicate to your examiner that you have been engaged in the development of your chosen skill to the same extent as your performing colleagues.

The theatre-design option is not an easy choice, and it does require a certain amount of performance from you, in that you must make a presentation of your ideas to your examiner before they are evidenced in the performance itself. Your presentation must last up to a maximum of ten minutes and needs to be structured in such a way as to allow your examiner to understand what you have been through in the preparation process and what you are expecting the examiner to see in relation to your design realised in the performance.

PREPARING FOR SECTION A

The individual skill is a challenge whatever it is you are going to do. We are now going to look at some possible ideas for theatre designers and suggestions of how you might approach your individual skill with the examiner in mind. Your design choice ideally should support a monologue or duologue offered by others in the group, and your presentation of ideas to the examiner should last no more than ten minutes. Whichever skill you choose for design in Section A, you must:

* prepare a concept to support your ideas;
* compile a portfolio to demonstrate your progress and understanding in relation to the complete play text;

• give a presentation to your examiner and realise your design in performance.

There is a lot to do here, particularly as there is a time limit on the monologue and duologue of two minutes and five minutes respectively. The demands on performance candidates to engage with the examiner within the time limit are very high; for a design candidate they are in some ways even more challenging, depending, of course, on your chosen design skill.

If you look at the specification, you will see that it gives you the opportunity to design for either a monologue or duologue or for another section of a play chosen for performance, possibly using other students to deliver the text. Caution is advised here. If we break this down for you, you can look at the specifics of what you need to do as a design candidate in Section A.

DESIGN FOR A MONOLOGUE

You would work with another member of your group to demonstrate your chosen skill in relation to a monologue lasting no more than two minutes. Think carefully about this in relation to the choice of design skills we set out at the start of this chapter in the overview of Unit 2 and as detailed on page 23 of the specification. Two minutes is not a great deal of time to demonstrate a performance skill, let alone to provide you with a reasonable platform to demonstrate your design in performance.

DESIGN FOR A DUOLOGUE

You would work with two other members of your group to demonstrate your chosen skill in relation to a duologue lasting no more than five minutes. Think carefully about this, again in relation to the choice of design skills we have already mentioned. Five minutes is not a great deal of time for two candidates to demonstrate a performance skill. It is also challenging for you if you are taking on the design skill option but possibly more viable for you than the monologue option.

DESIGN FOR A MONOLOGUE OR DUOLOGUE OF YOUR CHOICE

This is an option too but will mean that you need to find one or two performers to bring the extract to life for you in relation to your design skill. The advantage of this is that you will be in control and you can shape the performance in relation to your design. The disadvantage is that your chosen performers will not be assessed on their performance and, therefore, may not be as committed to the piece as you must be.

You could also be out on a limb as far as the rest of your teaching group is concerned, particularly if you are looking to use people from outside your group to assist you in this option. Probably the last thing you might want to do is to exclude yourself too much from the rest of your class, especially if it is your intention to take the course through the A2 year and you have to then pick up working with the group again on Unit 3. Whilst this option is offered in the specification and you are able to choose it if you wish, it really is worth considering the implications very carefully before setting off down this path.

CONSIDER YOUR OPTIONS

There is a lot for you to think about here. The theatre-design option is not here simply to accommodate those of you who do not wish to perform: it is here to encourage a positive and serious study of this important aspect of theatre and to encourage students opting for it to demonstrate how design can both shape a piece for performance and influence an audience's perception of it. Before making your decision, you may like to think about the following:

- Is there enough scope for me to develop my ideas in relation to the criteria grid?
- Is it challenging enough for me for this level of study?
- Am I able to access sufficient resources and materials to help me to realise my intentions?
- Will my design make a significant contribution to the monologue or duologue?
- How much influence will I have on the performer(s) in order for my contribution to be recognised in the performance?
- What do I hope to be able to achieve in Section A and will the design option enable me to do that?
- Do I know enough about the options to decide which design skill I want to offer?
- Will making a presentation of my ideas to the examiner be more daunting than preparing a monologue or a duologue?

When you consider each of the above points, you are not simply thinking about earning marks, but you would not be here if you did not have marks in mind when setting out on this specification. It may be worth considering very carefully the whole idea of offering this skill for Section A of Unit 2 and considering whether it is the right thing for you to be doing. Your teacher will have a view on this, and you really must be guided by that view. There is nothing to stop you offering design for either or both sections in this unit but, given the choice, could Section B offer you more scope for demonstrating your skills and earning you marks than Section A?

There is a wide choice of design elements that you can choose from, some of which may be more appealing than others. For Section A, you are looking at one design element only so you need to be very clear about two things:

1. Do you have sufficient access to materials and support in order for you to be able to fulfil the criteria?
2. Do you have sufficient skills to enable to you meet the practical requirements in order to access the full range of marks available for this option?

What we are going to do now is to take you through some of the ideas we have considered in relation to design for Section A in relation to a particular text. In doing this, we are assuming that you have a working knowledge of some of the terms we use in relation to design elements. We assume, for example, that you know what 'set and props' means. If this is not the case, then you need to be very seriously thinking about whether or not this option is for you, particularly if you are looking at this unit having spent the course so far exploring two texts for Unit 1 and possibly having already been involved in a theatre visit.

AN EYE FOR SHAPE AND COLOUR

As a design candidate, your view of theatre will be different in that you are looking at all of those elements of stagecraft which are there to support the actors, and you need to have a good eye for shape and colour and how particular effects combine to enhance the whole. You might find inspiration and ideas by looking at the Kneehigh and Frantic Assembly websites, both of which feature interesting and evocative production stills, indicating use of costume, set and a range of lighting states. We feature a number of images in this book, and each of those should tell you something about the use of design to enhance performance and may give you ideas for exploring design.

IDEAS AND UNDERSTANDING

As with the performance candidates in your group, you not only need to have ideas in relation to your design choice and the chosen extract but you also have to demonstrate an understanding of the play as a whole.

You may have been inspired by use of particular lighting effects in a production you have seen and would like to try to recreate those effects for Unit 2. This could be a good starting point, but there needs to be a clear understanding on your part of what is and is not possible in your school or college in relation to this. What is possible in your local theatre may not be possible in your drama studio. This does not mean you should not have a go but what it does mean is that you need to be guided in your decisions and in the approach you will have to meeting the criteria for demonstrating this skill for your examiner.

WORKED EXAMPLE

Kindertransport

Duologue 5 in the performance section (p. 120) is an extract from *Kindertransport,* and we will use this as the basis for looking at some possibilities for Section A design with you. There are challenges within this text for most of the design elements available for this section, but you would probably be looking at set or costume design in particular. The play is set in an attic room of a house in the 1980s but it also uses a **non-linear** structure in order to explore the character of 'Eva' and her transformation into 'Evelyn' from the 1930s up to the 1980s.

In the play, there are costume considerations for the actor playing 'Eva' as she ages into her teens and becomes 'English', for 'Lil' who is likely to be played by the same actor in both the past and the present, and for the representation of the rat-catcher. The attic room is a setting challenge and one that could give real opportunities for this section. It is certainly a play that requires a composite set and probably an imaginative use of lighting and sound to signify change in time and location, if you were considering design elements for a full production of it. As a design candidate, you need to demonstrate that you have a full understanding of the whole play and of how your design element would work in relation to an overall design concept, using the monologue or duologue to present a focused version of your ideas in order to demonstrate your wider understanding. For the purposes of this section within the examination, consider the following possibilities and how you might explore them.

non-linear
A play that has a structure that moves backwards and forwards in time in relation to the events unfolding for the audience.
It may start with the final scene and then go back to the beginning to show how the events unfolded to create this moment.

Set and props

The extract from *Kindertransport* lends itself to you creating for it a composite set that represents the attic room where the play is predominantly set. Your design ideas should indicate how you would explore the change in location and time in the play. Any exploration of set and props has to be undertaken with an understanding of scale, and you must be able to produce a scale ground plan and a scale model to reflect your ideas for the examiner. Full details of the requirements for this option are in the specification but if you are thinking of this as your option, then the extract from *Kindertransport* will provide you with an opportunity to explore and see how effectively this option will engage and challenge you.

There are essential elements you will need to include in your set and props design – boxes and their contents for Evelyn to search through, for example – but you will also need to consider how you represent this 'attic room' using other means too.

Costume

Lil as a character is present throughout the play and moves across the two main time periods of the piece. Your main consideration for costume design is how to enable the actress to move between the two time periods with very little opportunity for her to change in between some of the scenes. The full list of requirements for this option are in the specification, and you must consider these requirements carefully before embarking on this option. Exploring Lil may be an opportunity for you to be able to gauge whether or not this option is for you. You will need to research clothing from both the 1930s and the 1980s and to consider how you might indicate the passage of time for Lil as she goes through the Second World War with Eva and is represented in the play's present.

Lighting

There are lighting challenges for the attic in this play. It is not a dark and dusty attic but an attic room, so you may assume light sources from, for example, dormer windows or skylights as well as overhead lighting from artificial light sources. The lighting in this extract creates the ambience of the attic room, but the challenge in the play as a whole is to help to indicate the change in time and location as the play switches backwards and forwards in time. You will need to consider colour and how this may be used to help your audience recognise the change in location and time.

A contrast between 'now' and 'then' is relatively easy to achieve and to pinpoint for your audience. Look at the play text up to and including this extract and make some notes about how you might light these scenes to help your audience to recognise the change that takes place. You should be able to list decisions you might make about colour and say why particular colours may be used and to what effect. You might consider a particular lighting effect in order to indicate the dark presence of the Rat-catcher, and you need to be able to support your ideas with examples of your intentions in relation to the text as a whole but you will also recognise the fantasy nature of this character in contrast to the more naturalistic characters in the piece as a whole.

Extension Activity

The composite set

- Find out what is meant by 'composite set'. In your notebook, make a few sketches of a composite set for two of the duologues presented in the performance section. What other types of set and staging do you know? How familiar are you with the terms:

  - proscenium
  - thrust
  - traverse
  - promenade

- Draw your ideas for three different types of staging each for two of the duologues in the performance section.

Extension Activity

Costume design

Choose either play you have studied for Unit 1 and sketch ideas for costume for three of the central characters to demonstrate your understanding of how costume design fits into an overall design concept.

You should consider colour, texture and material in your ideas and be able to look at, for example, how costume can help audience to recognise not only the characters but also something about their personality and status as well. Prepare a five-minute presentation for your group to be given at a time specified by your teacher.

PREPARING FOR SECTION B

In Section B, the criteria for the theatre-design candidate is more or less the same except you will be working under the direction of your teacher who will prepare a concept for the production that will enable you to demonstrate your chosen design skill to the examiner.

There is probably an advantage in offering your design skill for the group performance. Your teacher will be directing this so will therefore be able to guide you more effectively and keep you on track in relation to the assessment criteria. Unlike Section A, you are able to choose more than one design option here if you wish, but you may need to think carefully about this in relation to the facilities available to you and, of course, in relation to your director's concept.

Page 24 of the current edition for the specification gives the choices, which are exactly the same as those for Section A. The marking structure is essentially the same except there are 10 marks available for your interpretation of the director's concept. A lot will depend on the text your teacher chooses for the group performance and then the interpretation of it.

If you are thinking of taking up this option, then you need to be talking to your teacher early on in the process. There is little point in wanting to explore costume if your teacher has an idea of presenting *The Crucible* in jeans and sweatshirts. Whilst this is an acceptable concept in itself, it would not offer a costume designer much scope to demonstrate skills at a level to be able to access the top range of marks for this section. If your teacher knows of your interest right at the start of the process, then it will not be too difficult to accommodate your ideas in any concept as long as there is access to materials and equipment in order for you to be able to meet the requirements. Your teacher really must guide you on this.

Given a choice between offering theatre design for Section A or Section B, a number of students may see the major advantage of looking at Section B rather than Section A. It could be a more inclusive experience for you being part of the performance group as designer than working largely on your own for Section A. You will have the director's interpretation to work with, and, presumably, there will be a more collective approach to ideas.

Figure 14.1
Costume. Although this group chose to wear white dungarees to symbolise their 'uniform', they each wore a different coloured T-shirt so that the examiner could identify them. See also Figure 13.2: the production of *Oh! What a Lovely War* had a very simple set with a screen to project images onto behind the actors.

Source: Alan Perks and Jacqueline Porteous.

CONCLUSIONS

There is a lot to think about here, and, certainly, you will need to discuss your options with your teacher. The option of offering design in this unit is not an easy one, but it could be very rewarding if you are the kind of student who is looking at the bigger picture of the drama and theatre experience beyond performance. We think that the options are clearly set out here and that we have probably steered you away from designing for Section A in favour of Section B. This is deliberate as we think Section B gives you more opportunity to develop your ideas but, like everything else, the final decision is between you and your teacher. Either way, the decision needs to be taken for the right reasons and to enable you to access the range of marks available for this unit.

Consider the information, talk to your teacher, and then make your decision. Once this has been done, you will probably have a very small window in which you can change your mind and opt for the performance skill instead. There is no shame in doing this, as long as you move quickly and positively. There are many talented design candidates involved in A-Level Drama and Theatre Studies, and their work is recognised equally alongside performance candidates in this specification. It could be you this year, but it does not have to be, not if you do not feel confident enough in being able to access the marks available to you through exploring this option.

15 The written concept

Whether you are performing or designing for Section A you must produce a written concept, which is sent to your examiner at least seven working days before your presentation. The specification uses the words 'rationale' and 'concept' for your written work to support your chosen skill in this section but we will try to be consistent here and use 'concept' to cover both words.

The written concept connects you, the extract and the original source material and should demonstrate an understanding of the complete text in order to justify your interpretation of it in the extract you have worked on as either performer or designer. This is not as daunting as it sounds, but there are aspects of this process that you must take seriously and be aware of *before* you start work on preparing your Section A skill.

The word limit of 500 is the maximum acceptable, and examiners will be expecting to see it as a maximum, not as a guideline figure. It states in the specification that the notes can be presented on one side of A3 or two sides of A4 and should typically include:

- evidence of an understanding of the complete text;
- acknowledgement of the context of the chosen monologue, duologue or design element within the complete play text;
- an explanation of the preparation process and the intended interpretation;
- for performers, an annotated copy of the text with justification of decisions made.

The phrase used on page 25 of the current edition of the specification is 'the written concept will typically include'. It therefore stands to reason that you will aim to follow the instructions very carefully and include information to cover all of these elements in your preparation notes which you can draw from to include in your final presented version for your examiner.

Five hundred words is not a lot, and it will probably be the case that you will need to be selective in the material you include in your final version of your written concept in order to meet the demands of the task and to access the word limit. If you are a performance student and you are including an annotated copy of your extract with your concept, it is likely to be the case that your annotation will count towards the 500 words of your concept. You will therefore need to send to the examiner:

- your 500-word (maximum to take into account any annotation) concept;
- your annotated copy of the extract you are performing.

We have mentioned more than once now that there is absolutely no point in exceeding word or time limits because anything over what is suggested in the specification will be ignored by your examiner. There will be absolutely no exceptions to this so it is important that you plan your work accordingly, and it might be worth referencing back to your work on Unit 1 and looking at how you were able to be selective in creating exploration notes of up to 3,000 words across the two texts.

Your written concept will be awarded a mark out of 10 by your examiner, from the total of 40 marks available for Section A and carries equal weighting to the other three elements of assessment in this section. It is therefore important that you prepare for this element of assessment in exactly the same way as you prepare for the others. It should be very straightforward, particularly if you have developed the discipline of keeping your notebook handy and of making notes of developments as you go along. Your examiner will read your concept before coming to examine your work, and it is your first point of contact, giving your examiner some indication of not only what you are doing but also how seriously you have taken the task of preparing for Section A, as represented by the way you have structured your concept. It is human nature that first impressions count for a lot, and your examiner needs to feel confident that you are well prepared for the demands of Unit 2.

The way you present your ideas will be taken into account by your examiner so you need to be absolutely clear about spelling, grammar and punctuation. If in doubt, ask! Your working notebook should contain all the information you will eventually include in your 500 words so use the note-taking as an opportunity to check your use of appropriate technical language and, of course, the way it is spelt.

Your examiner will use your 500 words to form an initial judgement of your understanding of your Section A material in relation to your understanding of the text as a whole. It is not enough to simply describe how you have created your character or design concept in relation to the extract; the concept needs to demonstrate an understanding of the text as a whole and the place of your extract within it. Evidence of a wider knowledge in relation to the text will be assessed within your concept. This is essentially the same whether you are a performance or design candidate.

WORKED EXAMPLE

Nights at the Circus

Consider the following concept in relation to the monologue from *Nights at the Circus* by Buffo the Clown. This has been written from a performance candidate's viewpoint but the piece lends itself very well to possible exploration in relation to costume or make-up. It is worth considering a couple of things while reading this concept:

- There are 489 words here. On the page it does not look like a lot but these 489 words have been distilled by the students from many more, and there are still areas that need a little more exploration in relation to the criteria. It is not a perfect example and lacks, for example, sufficient detail on the play as a whole.
- The tone of the concept is spot on. There is a real sense of the student in this rationale and a knowledgeable response to the demands of this task in relation to the preparation process and the interpretation.

This is just an example – one way of doing it – but the examiner will certainly pick up the confident use of appropriate vocabulary within the piece and will gain an insight into this interpretation before the day of the examination.

> I chose an extract from this play having seen Kneehigh's production. I was instantly struck by the power of this particular monologue. It is representative of many of the themes of the play. Most specifically, it shows the dark side of the circus, in this case clowning. This monologue can be interpreted from the text in different ways. I have decided that it is direct address to the audience and that I will treat the audience as that of a circus. I feel this gives the monologue another layer of irony. I chose the character of Buffo the Clown not only because I feel great empathy for this character's situation but also because during this speech his hidden depths are revealed. In the context of the whole play this is a poignant moment that I feel is captured beautifully within this short monologue.
>
> While rehearsing this monologue, I have had to consider how I want it to be communicated. Vocally, I try to portray a struggle within my character, of trying to appear upbeat with a clown-like tone, whilst fighting off evident pain in my voice. Owing to the nature

of the issues the clown is describing – death and failure – I feel my character cannot contain his emotions for long. In terms of movement, although I do not move around very much, I try to further develop the portrayal of an inner struggle through language. For example, I try to imagine I do not know what to do with my hands, therefore subconsciously wringing them and fidgeting. This is representative of something people do when nervous and talking about an awkward subject.

I have tried numerous rehearsal techniques in an effort to further the depth of the performance. For instance, I tried delivering it to an audience of two people, trying to maintain a realistic 'chatty' tone throughout. To do this, we engaged in normal conversation, and then after a short while and mid-flow I began the first line 'Let me tell you a story.' I tried to do this without breaking the syntax of the conversation, so that the text of my monologue was indistinguishable from the rest of the conversation. I felt that this exercise enabled me to develop a more personal and realistic feel to the piece.

In performance, my intention is to allow the audience to relate to the situation my character is in. I use different styles of phrasing at certain moments in order to evoke particular emotions in the audience. For example, I use a broken style of speech with lengthy pauses during the line 'and I froze. Like a baby gasping for air.' I aim to draw the audience's attention to the double meaning of this line, as I have just told of my wife giving birth to stillborn. This pause gives greater significance to the line, and I feel allows the audience to feel greater empathy for my character.

Figure 15.1
Buffo the Clown, *Nights at the Circus* (Kneehigh Theatre Company). © Steve Tanner.

This is one way of presenting the information. There will be other ways which your teacher may explore with you but, as part of the examination process, the final version of your concept must be your own work.

As with all material in this book, we are not suggesting you follow the example layout to the letter. What we have done is take the elements from the specification and present them in the model to show you the kind of information that could be included in your own work. Your teacher will have views on it, and, indeed, so will you, but our generic approach will hopefully guide you in the right direction, and, with the specification clearly at the centre of our thinking when preparing for examination, this could be a suitable way of organising your Unit 2 Section A rationale.

Another way of presenting the information is to take an A3 sheet. Take your extract and stick or photocopy it into the centre of your sheet and develop your concept around it to present a more visual approach to the task. There is an appeal to this, but you must be careful that you do not get so carried away with the presentation that you neglect the content. Your examiner will be looking beyond the presentation and searching out the content that hits the assessment criteria.

If you annotate your monologue by hand, surround this with your contextualisation of the piece, print it and then stick it onto the A3 sheet, then the examiner will be able to separate your 500 words (maximum) from your preparation of the speech itself. This approach will not work for duologues as these will tend to be longer and will therefore take up too much space on an A3 sheet. As a guide to what this might look like though for a monologue, there is an example of an annotated section from a text in Figure 8.1 (pp. 34–5), and this may be an approach you want to explore further to adapt it for this unit. The Exam Board may have rules concerning the presentation of your notes, and an A3 sheet may fall outside those rules, so it is always best for you to go with whatever information your teacher has access to in relation to this. Updates will be posted at regular intervals on the website and our blog.

It is important not to underestimate the importance of the written concept, and you need to ensure that it serves its purpose in engaging with the examiner before the day of the performance – but in a way that is succinct and focused. With the example from *Nights at the Circus* in mind, have a look at the essential requirements that follow.

WRITTEN-CONCEPT REQUIREMENTS: SECTION A

Performance

Your teacher will probably go through this with you, but, very simply, this is an examined component of the unit and is worth a quarter of your marks (10/40) for Section A. If nothing else, this is an opportunity to connect your ideas around your approach to your extract to the examiner in a positive way before the day of the practical examination. One of the purposes of the concept is to encourage you to select the monologue, duologue or design skill from a position of a broader understanding of the text, or, if the monologue, duologue or design skill comes first, then it will encourage you to demonstrate an understanding of the play as a whole. You cannot simply select a monologue and perform it: you need to demonstrate an understanding of its context. Look at the concept for Buffo the Clown again. The 500 words is a maximum, but it should represent your considered response to the text as a whole and reflect your understanding through the way you select information that is appropriate to include in the concept to support your performance. There is no need to be over-fanciful, nor to make claims for your intended performance that will be blatantly untrue. Keep it factual but also consider the quality of written communication too.

Your teacher will be around and will guide you in appropriate ways, keeping an overview of the group and your individual contribution within it to hopefully keep you on track too as you head towards the deadlines for submitting the concept. The examiner will be looking at the concept in relation to:

- evidence of understanding of the complete play text;
- acknowledgement of the context of the chosen extract;
- an explanation of the preparation process and intended interpretation.

The word limit will soon be reached, so preparation and structuring is vital. The selection of material will help the examiner to gain an insight into the intended presentation or performance, should be focused mainly on your experience in preparing the piece and is not intended to be a scholarly exploration of the art of the playwright in its historical context. Your understanding of the context will be important, and you will recognise this in the concept, but this will primarily be demonstrated in the performance or presentation of your design skill itself. Consider the following as examples of approaches to structuring a concept:

- text;
- context;
- process.

Interpretation/performance

This may help with the structure of the concept and will set it out on the page in a way that is easily accessible for the examiner. Each of these sub-headings is developed in a paragraph in your concept.

As we have mentioned, the 500-word maximum does not give a great deal of room for manoeuvre, and you need to be really careful that you keep within the structure. A more personal response to the experience could engage the examiner. Look at the following extracts from a concept. For example:

- I relished the opportunity of exploring Joey's speech from Act 1 of *Road,* having seen and read the play and recognised the challenge there was in the speech for an actor, particularly working with CC as Clare.
- Although *Road* was written over twenty years ago, I can see that people today will recognise the damaged characters in our duologue and the debate the play opens up about the destruction of society in the 1980s with no thought of the individual.
- My portrayal of Joey has an edgy modern feel to it, almost like he is high on drugs but he is high on his need to create his own society in his bedroom for him and Clare. I want the audience to be shocked and moved at this moment in the play. I also want them to wonder where the relationship with Clare is going. One of the ways I will do this particularly is in my physicality. I will draw spirals and squares on my arms.

Within this kind of structure, you would be demonstrating a wider knowledge of the text and starting to develop the concept in the direction of contextualising the chosen extract. This kind of response also has immediacy about it, even though it has been distilled from pages of notes in the working notebook. Notice how it includes 'CC' who is playing Clare in the duologue but does not dwell on her. 'CC' will have her own concept to write, and there will be overlap between the two, but this is an individual response to the challenge.

You may prefer the more structured approach of having sub-headings in order to set out your responses. This could be a sensible approach to this task. It may be that you work within the sub-headings as you go along and then take away the framework for your final version. The examiner will be looking at content more than structure, so as long as the approach allows for content to be presented to demonstrate an outstanding response to the chosen play, and a comprehensive account of both the preparation process and the intended interpretation, then whatever you present will be assessed by the examiner.

Design

This will be familiar if you have been working your way through this section of the book and have just read the information for performance candidates. Just like for your performance colleagues this is an examined component of the unit and is worth a quarter of the marks (10/40) available for Section A. It is important as it gives you an opportunity to connect to the examiner in a positive way before the day of the practical examination and sets up your presentation/demonstration.

One of the purposes of the concept is to encourage you to be careful in your selection of the theatre-design skill you are offering in this section but also its selection in relation to the monologue or duologue you are supporting. You are looking to demonstrate a wider knowledge of the text and your approach to it in your concept.

As we have mentioned, the 500 words is a maximum but it should represent your considered response to the text as a whole and reflect your understanding through the selection of information that is appropriate to include in the concept to support your theatre-design skill in its realisation.

Your teacher will be there in support and will keep you on track with the requirements of this section and the deadlines you are working towards. The most appropriate approach to the theatre design skill will probably be to go for a design option for a duologue chosen by two other members of your group, giving you more scope for developing ideas. The choice of play is very important, probably as important as the candidates you choose to work with on creating your design as you must have an opportunity to access up to 30 per cent of the marks for your AS course through demonstrating this skill.

The examiner will be looking at your rationale to support the interpretation, preparation and final demonstration. This should include:

- an overall design concept for the complete play text;
- a rationale of the final design decisions.

Remember, in addition to the concept, you will produce other written evidence to support your ten-minute (maximum) presentation to the examiner. It is important that your concept indicates the thinking behind the ideas presented, and there should be as little overlap as possible.

The word limit will soon be reached – look at the Buffo the Clown example – so preparation and structuring is vital. Your selection of information will help the examiner to gain an insight into the intended presentation and demonstration, and you should probably focus mainly on the experience of developing and using the design skill. The concept is not intended to be a scholarly exploration of the art of the playwright in its historical context, nor the generic role of the designer in theatre. It is about you responding to the extract and to the play in relation to the skill you are demonstrating.

The grid on page 31 of the current edition of the specification clearly indicates the requirements for this section, and these will form the basis for assessment by the examiner. It is important that you look carefully at the list and choose both the skill and the performance piece with an eye on being able to meet these basic requirements. There may be more of a challenge here than you might at first have thought. *Road,* by Jim Cartwright, for example, offers opportunities under most of the headings, with setting and props being an obvious choice.

WORKED EXAMPLE

Road by Jim Cartwright

My ideas for setting are centred around the bed that must be really important in this scene. TM and CC want to have a sense that Joey is creating his own society in his bedroom for him and Clare. I want the audience to be shocked and moved at this moment in the play, and I want the setting to support the characters as much as possible. One of the influences I have drawn on is Tracey Emin's artwork *My Bed*. I want the actors to be able to move within the space but also to have a real sense of belonging – particularly Joey as it is his room. One way of I am hoping to achieve this is . . .

Within this kind of structure, you would be demonstrating a wider knowledge of the text and starting to develop your concept in the direction of contextualising the chosen extract and design skill. This kind of response also has immediacy about it, even though you have distilled it from pages of notes in your working notebook. You may prefer the more structured sub-headings approach in order to set out your responses, and it could be an interesting and valuable planning exercise to work within the sub-headings as you go along and then take away the framework to see how you respond. It is up to you, but the sub-headings may give you a structure and may guide your examiner into your thinking more effectively. The examiner will be looking at the content rather than the structure so keep it clear and simple and see this as an opportunity to engage your examiner with your ideas before he or she sees your work.

As a design-skills candidate, you will need to produce a concept for Section B too if you choose to offer design for the group piece. This concept will be very similar to the one for Section A, with the major difference being that you will be working within your teacher's directorial concept for the group performance.

WRITTEN-CONCEPT REQUIREMENTS: SECTION B

Design

It is essential that you have access to your director's interpretation throughout the preparation process in order for your design to reflect the style, genre and overall demands of the final production.

The starting point of the Unit 2 Section B production is the script. Your director is responding to the script to create a performance that meets the requirements of the unit and the expected audience at your centre. You need to be aware of the decisions made as part of the overall planning process in order to be able to reflect them in the chosen design element(s) and in the written design documentation and design concept (sent to the examiner seven days before the performance).

You need to be aware of the style, genre and overall demands of the production if you are going to be able to reflect them in your design ideas. You must engage the examiner through the written design concept that sets the scene for your presentation and the realisation of design in the performance on the day of the examination. It could be that your opening sentence in the written design concept could set out your understanding of the director's interpretation as follows:

> Our director wanted to create an ensemble feel for this production of Macbeth and decided to focus on the witches with actors multi-roling from the ensemble. My costume designs have to take into account the needs for unity but also an opportunity for quick changes for all actors when playing central characters as well.

There is an immediate connection here between you and the examiner, and there is understanding demonstrated in a succinct and clear way. There is also a confidence here, evident in the use of language – ensemble, multi-roling, unity. The examiner immediately knows something about the interpretation, supported by the director's interpretation which will be sent at the same time, and something about your chosen design element. For example:

> Colour and texture are important in this interpretation, and I had to take it into account when designing the costumes for all of the witches but particularly for SB who is multi-roling as Lady Macbeth. The two colour schemes of dark blues and purples (witches) and earth colours (others) have to provide contrast and signals for the audience but they must also be interchangeable at times to help the actors to change quickly as some need to do at times – Lady Macbeth and Macbeth at one point in a matter of seconds . . .

This development of the idea from this candidate looks at the importance of colour, is clearly in response to the director's interpretation and may go on to contextualise the costumes in relation to the overall style of the piece and other colours of settings and use of light, for example, that may be used by the director, indicating the integration of the work of the designer into the whole. Whatever your design skill is, you should not see it in isolation. It must form part of the bigger picture of the performance and be integrated into it. For example:

> This interpretation of Macbeth is very physical. As a company, we have worked with the director on **physical theatre** and this has been a real influence on the production. I was really aware of the need for freedom of movement in my designs and had to be very careful that my costumes are practical for the performance and the promenade style with varying levels that are used in the production. They also need to be easy for the actors to change in and out of. A good example of this you will see is . . .

physical theatre
A term from the late twentieth century to mean an approach to performance that uses highly developed physical skills to represent character and situation, with actors often representing location as well as characters in the performance.

This kind of paragraph would indicate your understanding of the overall demands of the production, not the play but the interpretation by your teacher-director. The production places particular demands on costume, the multi-roling and the style of performance, for example, and you would be acknowledging this here. The concept may indicate particular aspects of costume that you would like the examiner to look for during the performance, but this is more likely to be mentioned in more detail during the presentation. In a way, your concept is like the introduction to what is to follow on the day of the examination, but it should also show an understanding of the way in which the costumes will complement the overall impact of the production. There needs to be a confidence here that the examiner will notice in both the structure of the concept and your use of language that is appropriate to the skills being detailed. For example:

> This has been a great learning experience for me, and I am looking forward to seeing my designs in action during the performance. The challenge of creating practical ideas and seeing them become a reality while recognising the needs of individuals in the company has been a major driving force for me in designing the costumes for this interpretation of Macbeth.

INTERPRETATION OF DIRECTOR'S CONCEPT

It is possible in this section for a theatre-design candidate to offer more than one design skill for examination. You might consider linking two skills together. Lighting and sound, or costume and make-up, for example, could be obvious combinations, and the grid on page 31 of the specification sets out the minimum requirements you have to meet should you be considering more than one skill. It is probably the case, however, that the majority of candidates for this option will focus on one design skill and develop it appropriately within their director's interpretation.

It could be good practice for the director to support the work of the design-skills candidate in the director's written concept and point both the examiner and you in the right direction when it comes to the 500-word concept you will send to the examiner seven days before the day of the performance.

Essentially, the concept for Section B is the same as for Section A and could be structured in a similar way. The most important difference is that it is supporting the work of the director, rather than the approach of the monologue or duologue students and, as such, needs to marry with what the director writes in his or her interpretation. There is more ground for you to cover as a designer in this section, looking at your chosen design skill in relation to up to sixty minutes, rather than up to five minutes, but an understanding of the play as a whole and of your response within the director's interpretation need to be evident in the concept.

This will inform the examiner of the kind of areas to be covered in your presentation and, more importantly, in the performance itself. Your concept will pave the way for your presentation that is supported by a portfolio of research and sketches showing the development of ideas and your interpretation of the director's concept. Have a look at the following examples from possible concepts.

WORKED EXAMPLE

Working with my director on his interpretation of *Our Country's Good* by Timberlake Wertenbaker, I relished the challenge of recreating costumes from the period and particularly focused on colour in relation to groups of characters and the contrast our director wanted to create between the officers and the convicts.

These few lines immediately connect the candidate and the director and indicate for the examiner specific areas that should be developed during the presentation and the performance itself. The examiner will note:

- period;
- colour;
- officers and convicts.

There is immediacy here from the candidate that gives a real sense of confidence in the approach to costume, and this, in turn, implies understanding that should be developed during the presentation.

The candidate could then set out an understanding of the context of the play and an interpretation covering approach to costume in relation to the grid on page 31 of the specification. This should support what the examiner is going to hear and see on the day of the examination in relation to the costumes for *Our Country's Good*. It will also indicate an understanding of the piece that is in tune with the director's interpretation, in the same way as the performance candidates are in tune with it. Sketches and diagrams in the portfolio should visually expand on these ideas.

WORKED EXAMPLE

When I spoke to my director I realised that there was a real challenge to creating costume for the character of Ralph Clark. The actor is the only one not playing more than one character but spends all of the play as RC so I had to be careful to make sure that the costume was both representative of his role within the piece but also practical in that he needs to wear it – or variations of it – throughout the sixty minutes of performance. Some early sketches were based on research I did. I looked at *The Fatal Shore* by Robert Hughes and found out more about the real people and historical events that Wertenbaker based these characters on.

The examiner will note:

- costume research;
- practical;
- sketches.

The candidate in this example focuses on Ralph Clark and goes into the kind of detail that will be expanded upon in the presentation on the day of the examination. It seems as though there are a number of skills here to keep you focused. It is therefore important that you work alongside the director and have a clear understanding of the complete play text as well as the interpretation to be presented for examination.

You also need to demonstrate an awareness of how the design skill will affect the audience within the performance. All of this information will be gathered by you during the process, recorded and then distilled into concept, documentation and presentation. This is then available in your portfolio which should form the basis for both your concept and your presentation to the examiner.

Of course, you may have a different approach to this. You may, for example, start your concept and your presentation with, 'Our Country's Good by Timberlake Wertenbaker is a play about . . . It was written in the 1980s and reflects particular anxieties of the time about . . . Our director's inter-pretation focuses on . . . My approach to costume is . . . This will be shown through . . . , etc.'

There is more of a mechanical approach to this structure, but it may also allow you to access the outstanding mark bands in the assessment grid. What is probably the most important thing to remember as a design-skills candidate is to make the connection across both the written elements, the diagram-matical elements and the realisation of your design in performance.

Your concept sets out for your examiner what will be presented on the day of the examination. You will have up to ten minutes to present your ideas to the examiner, and your ideas will be supported by the portfolio you have compiled as you have gone along. Your examiner will need to see your portfolio, and there is a mark awarded for this as well.

FURTHER READING AND RESOURCES FOR PARTS II AND III

Plays

Beckett, Samuel (1953) *Waiting for Godot,* London: Faber and Faber.
Berkoff, Steven (1989) *Decadence,* London: Faber and Faber.

—— (1988) *The Trial*, Charlbury: Amber Lane Press.

—— (1989) *West*, London: Faber and Faber.

—— (2002) *Requiem for Ground Zero*, Charlbury: Amber Lane Press.

Bond, Edward (1991) *The War Plays Trilogy*, London: Methuen.

—— (1973) *The Sea*, London: Methuen.

Brecht, Bertolt (2007) *The Caucasian Chalk Circle*, London: Penguin.

—— (1986) *Mother Courage*, London: Methuen.

Cartwright, Jim (1991) *Two*, London: Methuen.

—— (1986) *Road*, London: Methuen.

Churchill, Caryl (1984) *Fen*, London: Samuel French.

—— (1985) *Vinegar Tom*, London: Routledge.

D'Angelis, April (1994) *Playhouse Creatures*, London: Samuel French.

Farquhar, George (1991) *The Recruiting Officer*, London: Methuen.

Genet, Jean (1954) *The Maids*, New York: Grove Press.

Gogol, Nikolai (1985) *The Government Inspector*, London: Methuen.

Ibsen, Henrik (1985) *A Doll's House*, London: Methuen.

Kane, Sarah (2000) *4:48 Psychosis*, London: Methuen.

Karge, Manfred (1988) *Man to Man*, London: Methuen.

Littlewood, Joan (1965) *Oh! What a Lovely War*, London: Methuen.

Lorca, Federico García (1996) *Blood Wedding*, London: Faber and Faber.

Marber, Patrick (1997) *Closer*, London: Methuen.

Pinter, Harold (1991) *The Birthday Party*, London: Faber.

—— (1988) *Mountain Language*, London: Faber.

Potter, Dennis (1984) *Blue Remembered Hills*, London: Samuel French.

Priestley, J. B. (1948) *An Inspector Calls*, London: Samuel French.

Samuels, Diane (1995) *Kindertransport*, London: Nick Hern Books.

Shakespeare, William, *Macbeth* various.

Sophocles (1984) *The Theban Plays*, Harmondsworth: Penguin.

Wertenbaker, Timberlake (1995) *Our Country's Good*, London: Methuen.

—— (1989) *The Love of a Nightingale*, London: Faber.

Wilde, Oscar (1995) *The Importance of Being Earnest*, London: Penguin.

PRACTITIONERS FOR PERFORMANCE AND DESIGN

Artaud, Antonin (1970) *The Theatre and its Double*, London: Calder.

Berkoff, Steven (1977) *Free Association*, London: Faber and Faber.

Billington, Michael (1996) *The Life and Work of Harold Pinter*, London: Faber and Faber.

Carnicke, Sharon (2008) *Stanislavsky in Focus*, London: Routledge.

Craig, Edward Gordon (2008) *On The Art of the Theatre*, London: Routledge.

—— (1983) *Craig on Theatre*, London: Methuen.

Eyre, Richard and Wright, Nicholas (2000) *Changing Stages: A View of British and American Theatre in the Twentieth Century*, London: Bloomsbury.

Fo, Dario (1987) *The Tricks of the Trade*, London: Methuen.

Goodwin, John (1989) *British Theatre Design*, London: Weidenfeld and Nicolson.

Graham, Scott and Hoggett, Steven (2009) *The Frantic Assembly Book of Devising Theatre*, London: Routledge.

Griffiths, Trevor R. (1982) *Stagecraft*, London: Phaidon.

Lecoq, Jacques (2002) *The Moving Body*, London: Methuen.

Marowitz, Charles (1999) *The Other Way: An Alternative Approach to Acting and Directing*, London and New York: Applause.

Mitchell, Katie (2008) *The Director's Craft*, London: Routledge.

Scheer, Edward (2001) *Antonin Artaud: A Critical Reader*, London: Routledge.

Shevtsova, Maria (2007) *Robert Wilson*, London: Routledge.

Stanislavsky, Konstantin (1999) *An Actor's Handbook*, London: Methuen.

—— (2008) *An Actor's Work*, London: Routledge.

Whelan, Jeremy (1994) *Instant Acting*, Cincinatti, Ohio: Betterway Books.

Wilsher, Toby (2006) *The Mask Handbook*, London: Routledge.

MOVING ON

PART IV

16 Looking ahead to the A2 year

This section will bring the AS year to a close by both reflecting on some of the experiences we have had so far and looking forward to the A2 year and Units 3 and 4. Part of the approach to looking forward that your teacher may take with you is to do some planning and preparation for the A2 year in the final half term of the AS year. This is seen as good practice, and it may be that it will give you confidence to look ahead to the new year with the knowledge that the challenges ahead will engage you in creating approaches to performance which are fitting for this level of study. There is no doubt that the A2 year will stretch your understanding of how drama and theatre works, but, perhaps more importantly, it will test your developmental skills as a deviser and as a director.

Unit 3 is about creating an original piece of theatre from a given source, and Unit 4 is about you responding to a given text and theatrical time period from the position of a director and as an informed member of an audience.

Your teacher may help to prepare you for the A2 year at the end of the AS year in one or more of the following ways.

DEVISING PERFORMANCES

There may be an opportunity for you to **devise** performances with a specific audience in mind, creating theatre to a brief either from your teacher or from another body or organisation, for example a local primary school looking for work on road safety for Years 5 and 6.

devising
Creating performance from a given stimulus, usually a collaborative process for actors.

PRACTITIONERS IN PRACTICE

Again, with Unit 3 in mind, your teacher may set you the task of researching and presenting a piece of work on a given theme or arising from a stimulus in the style of a practitioner other than any you may have looked at specifically as part of the course so far.

HISTORICAL RESEARCH

Your teacher may set a project for you to research one of the given time periods for Unit 4 and give you a time limit, after which you need to present your findings to the rest of your group. Your teacher may set this task for you in twos or threes, depending on the total numbers in your class.

BACKGROUND READING AND PREPARING AN EXTRACT FOR PERFORMANCE

With Unit 4 in mind, your teacher may set you extracts from one of the possible three texts you may study for that unit, with the aim of helping you to be more familiar with the texts and to help you to have a better understanding of the performance demands you may be faced with when looking at the texts to help you prepare for the final unit of the course. Versions of the texts for Unit 4 are available from Edexcel, and your teacher will probably have downloaded a copy of each in order to have a look at them before making a final decision about which one to choose for you to work with. All three texts are challenging theatrically, which is why they have been prepared for you for this examination.

THEATRE VISIT

You may have the opportunity to go on a theatre visit in preparation for the A2 year. Some schools and colleges arrange two or three day trips to see a variety of performances in order to help students to gain a better understanding of how directors will approach a range of texts in order to bring them to life for an audience. All of these activities may be arranged for you at the end of the AS year to help you to think about moving on. If they are not, then treat these examples as extension activities and set out a programme of study for yourself to help you to prepare for Units 3 and 4. There is nothing to stop you or others in your group from arranging your own theatre trips, independent of your teacher and covering a range of performances. It may not be as expensive as you might think. You cannot move on without a period of reflection, and some of that will inevitably happen once your results for the AS year are available. We hope that you will have achieved the UMS (uniform mark scale – for each unit as AS) points you are looking for in order to encourage you to go on to the A2 year, if that is your intention. Your teacher will become more of a guiding figure in the A2 year, giving you opportunities to use the skills you have developed during the

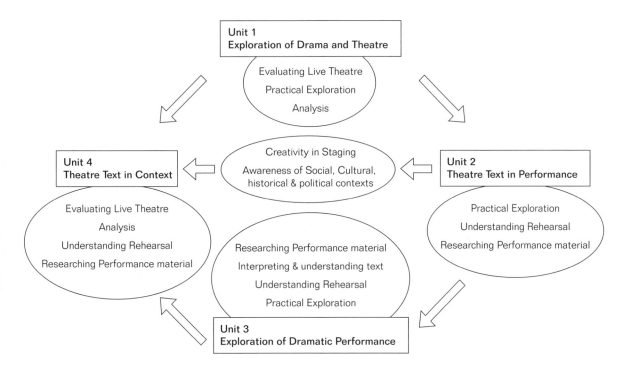

Unit 1
Exploration of Drama and Theatre

Evaluating Live Theatre

Practical Exploration

Analysis

Unit 4
Theatre Text in Context

Creativity in Staging

Awareness of Social, Cultural, historical & political contexts

Unit 2
Theatre Text in Performance

Evaluating Live Theatre

Analysis

Understanding Rehearsal

Researching Performance material

Practical Exploration

Understanding Rehearsal

Researching Performance material

Researching Performance material

Interpreting & understanding text

Understanding Rehearsal

Practical Exploration

Unit 3
Exploration of Dramatic Performance

course to date in order for you to be able to access the criteria for assessment in the second year.

There will be teaching that will enable your learning to take place, but a lot of the decisions you will have to make will be your decisions, rather than those put forward by your teacher. You need to be confident that you are able to work in a more guided structure than in a heavily directed one. Have a look around you again. Those people sitting around you are going to support you in getting the grade you want from this course, and you will be doing the same for them. With this in mind, you are now ready to move on to the A2 year. Our companion book to this one is also available with a wealth of ideas to guide you through the A2 year and, if you have not already done so, you might want to visit the website and find out a little more about Drama and Theatre Studies. Good luck!

Figure 16.1
Skills from each unit develop across the AS and A2 level.

Glossary of useful words and phrases

The following glossary is made up of drama and theatre words, most of which appear throughout this book. If you got to this point, you are probably familiar with many of these words already. This list is to help you to develop your own understanding of some of the more commonly used words and phrases you may come across on this course. The focus is mainly on those words and phrases we look at in Unit 1 and Unit 2, but there are some more generic words included here too.

A glossary is not a dictionary or an encyclopedia, so we do not, for example, include theatrical people or places here. You will have come across some useful information in the book and, if this has set you thinking about a particular person, play or place, then there are numerous websites that you could access in order to extend your knowledge – a list of some of these is also included at the end of the book. There is also a list of suggested further reading and viewing – not an exhaustive list, but one which should prove accessibly to you at this level of study and one to which you and your teacher can add alternative texts and films that you may come across as part of the course.

The glossary signals for you where your thinking should lie in terms of being aware of the use of the language of drama and theatre at this level of study and, perhaps more importantly, how to spell it and what it means!

Building a subject-specific vocabulary is something that will become very personal as your knowledge develops and it is useful to be able to recognise drama and theatre terms as they occur.

apron
In a traditional proscenium-arch theatre, the section of stage that projects in front of the curtain.

auditorium
Where the audience sits. In traditional theatres, the audience and performers are separated by a curtain.

back story
A back story is a relatively new term that provides a history for a character.

black box
A performance space that has no distinguishing features to define space for audience and performers and is extremely flexible. This is usually painted black, with black curtaining and is a typical studio space, often used for workshops as well as for performances.

blackout
When the lights go off to create complete darkness in a performance, usually to indicate the end of a scene, a change of mood and time or place or the end of the performance.

blocking
The defining by the director of the actor's moves and positioning on stage usually early on in the rehearsal process and in relation to how the piece will eventually look for the audience.

box set
A set that consists of three walls around a proscenium-arch stage with the proscenium opening as the fourth wall of the 'box'. The audience is looking into the world of the characters. Often this is seen as a traditional approach to defining space for the performance and a location for the audience.

cast
As a verb to assign roles to the actors. The cast is the list of characters in the play and the names of the actors playing them.

chronological
Something that is presented in order of the events as they occur in time.

cue
The line on which an actor should enter the scene or move to a different position or get ready to speak his line. In technical terms, a line at which an effect must happen, for example a change in light, sound effect or element of staging.

cyclorama
Usually white fabric which covers the entire back wall of the stage and onto which images can be projected or colour lighting effects portrayed.

designer
Responsible for creating the look and feel of the production. There are usually a number of contributors to design in the professional theatre, each responsible for a particular aspect of design, including set, lighting and costume.

devising
Creating performance from a given stimulus, usually a collaborative process for actors.

director

The person in control of all aspects of the production, primarily in relation to the actors but also responsible for the ideas to inspire the design considerations to support the overall vision. Most directors will work collaboratively but will exercise the right to have the final say.

doubling

An actor taking on two roles within the performance – doubling up.

downstage

The area of a traditional stage nearest to the audience.

dress rehearsal

Usually the rehearsal just before the first performance when everybody must wear full costume. The dress rehearsal is as close as possible to the actual performance without an audience present (usually!). It is often combined with a technical rehearsal where any effects and lighting or sound cues are tested and perfected to see that they work under performance conditions.

DSL

Downstage left (stage direction).

DSR

Downstage right (stage direction).

Elizabethan theatre

From the time period of Queen Elizabeth I – usually associated with Shakespeare and Marlowe, but other influential playwrights were also at work during this period.

emotion memory

Stanislavskian rehearsal technique in which actors are encouraged to draw on past experiences to help develop their relationship with their character.

epic theatre

A term from Brecht in which major world events are seen through the eyes of individuals.

episodic

A play written in short scenes or episodes that help create an almost cinematic feel for the performance and encourages a fast-paced production.

examiner

The person who will come to apply the national standard to work presented for examination purposes.

exposition

The means by which the plot of the play unfolds.

flat

An oblong frame of timber, covered with either canvas or hardboard and painted to help represent a location. A number of flats could create a room for a box set, for example, or a forest scene if painted appropriately and situated around the acting area.

flood

A lantern that gives a wide-spreading unfocused beam of light. This is very useful for general coverage, particularly if lighting equipment is limited or the effect you are hoping to achieve is minimalist.

follow-spot

A focused beam of light, either hand operated or, more usually, electronically controlled that can pinpoint and follow an actor within a space to create a specific isolating effect to focus the audience's attention on that character. Most often a follow spot is used in musical theatre and concerts.

fourth wall, the

In relation to the traditional proscenium arch, the opening of the arch is often referred to as the fourth wall, with the audience looking through it into the life of the characters. Characters can be confined by the fourth wall – they don't look out at the audience – or they can break the fourth wall, step through the arch and look at the audience and, in some plays, address them directly.

fresnel

A type of spotlight that has a lens of concentric ridged rings and projects a variable angle soft-edged beam.

FX effects

Usually sound effects in the theatre.

improvising

Exploring character and situation to gain a greater understanding of the who, why and where of the relationships. Sometimes leads to performance but often used as a means of supporting more developed work around scripts.

in the round

A performance space in which the audience is seated around the actors with a performance taking place in the middle.

In Yer Face Theatre

A term coined in the latter part of the twentieth century to group together plays by Patrick Marber, Sarah Kane and others to define the style and content as extremely challenging for the audience. Nothing was merely hinted at in these plays; it was all up front and on display, often in gory expletive detail.

interpretation

The approach to a text a director will adopt to create a version of the play in performance that has a particular stamp on it. Look at the work of Katie Mitchell, for example.

Jacobean

Of the period of King James I of England and following on from the Elizabethan period.

kitchen-sink drama

A term coined in the late 1950s to mean plays that represented a slice of working-class domestic life as seen in the work of John Osborne, for example.

left

Stage left, or the left-hand side as you face the audience. In traditional theatre, also called the prompt side.

lighting designer

Responsible for designing, focusing and plotting the lighting for the production, working in close cooperation with the director.

melodrama

A style of performance developed in the latter half of the nineteenth century which had a major influence on the early days of British cinema. Melodramas were known for their 'stock' characters of villain, heroine and hero, and they were often based on real-life characters – William Corder and his murder victim, Maria Marten, for example.

moderator

The person appointed by the Examination Board to ensure that work from your centre has been marked in line with the national standard.

Morality plays

Plays that had a strong moral content, that taught the audience something, e.g. *Everyman*.

Mystery plays

Plays that tell the story of the Christian calendar, dated from around the fifteenth century.

naturalism

Representation in performance which is as close as possible to real life.

non-linear

A play that has a structure that moves backwards and forwards in time in relation to the events unfolding for the audience. It may start with the final scene and then go back to the beginning to show how the events unfolded to create this moment.

notes
The director's observations usually during final rehearsals and first performances to help the company to fine-tune the performance based on audience response.

physical theatre
A term from the late twentieth century to mean an approach to performance that uses highly developed physical skills to represent character and situation, with actors often representing location as well as characters in the performance.

physicality
An actor's ability to embody a character by use of movement and gesture.

plot
The story of the drama – what happens to who and why.

pre-life
A Stanislavskian technique of looking at what was going on in the life of a character before the events of the play, used to help an actor gain a greater understanding of why a character may react in a particular way in the life of the play.

pre-set
The stage space as set before the production starts and what the audience sees when the curtains open or the lights go up.

promenade
A style of theatre in which the audience moves amongst the action that takes place within a defined space with minimal props and that looks back at the medieval performances in town centres and through city streets. Promenade demands real commitment from the audience and control from the actors in order to direct the audience's attention towards where the next scene is going to take place.

properties or **props**
Small items that an actor will carry on stage in order to help define character for the audience. Usually includes set dressing too.

proscenium
The traditional picture-frame type of stage, usually – but not always – with a curtain. The audience look through the arch to the actors who are separated from them by the frame. This type of staging is usually, but not always, associated with the box set.

proscenium arch
The actual opening of the frame itself, which often forms the boundary between performers and audience, particularly in more traditional theatre with performers not stepping outside it during the performance.

proxemics
Establishing relationships between actors and between actors and audience through exploring stage positioning and usually defined during the blocking process of rehearsal.

rake
The angle of slope from upstage to downstage in a traditional theatre space. The slope was originally included for better sightlines, in effect tilting the stage towards the audience so they could see better. Some rakes were so steep in some theatres that they created a real challenge for set builders. Most modern theatres have the audience banked rather than the stage which tends to be looked down on by the audience in a traditional Greek style.

rig
A lighting term to mean to set the lights in position. The word is also used to mean the finished positioning of the lantern – the rig.

right
The right-hand side of the stage as the actor looks at the audience.

rostrum
A platform, both moveable or fixed that raises the action above floor level.

set
The scenery for a production or for a particular scene.

set dressing
Items within the set to indicate the location for the audience – a tree stump with a shotgun leaning against it, for example.

sightlines
Can all of the audience see everything within the performance space that they need to see?

site-specific
a performance that takes place in a location that is reflected somehow within the piece itself – a Georgian house under renovation, for example, may provide an opportunity for site-specific work looking at the generations of families who have lived there.

technical rehearsal
Often combined with the dress rehearsal. An opportunity to go through all of the technical elements to make sure that everything works as it should do as close as possible to the performance but giving enough time to work on things that may cause concern.

Theatre of Cruelty

The theatre of Antonin Artaud. A forerunner of In Yer Face Theatre that challenges the audience on every level and sets out to make them think about the human condition. Artaud's use of the word 'cruelty' needs further exploration as it encompasses a range of ideas for performers and designers as well as audience.

thought tracking

A rehearsal technique that involves actors speaking the inner thoughts of characters in order to indicate a level of understanding behind the lines.

thrust stage

A stage that comes out into the audience that creates a platform for the actors very close to the audience. Traditionally this is associated with the Globe Theatre.

Total Theatre

Associated with Physical Theatre and arising from the work of, amongst others, Steven Berkoff. Total Theatre immerses the actor completely in the exploration of physical representation of character and situation.

tragedy

A style of theatre stemming from Ancient Greece and developed through the centuries by playwrights, most famously Shakespeare, in which the protagonist or hero suffers serious misfortune, usually as a result of human and divine actions.

traverse

A performance space in which the audience sit in rows facing each other with the action taking place down the centre of the space between them.

trebling

Taking on three roles within a performance.

upstage

The area towards the back of the acting area, away from the audience. Called upstage because of its association with raked theatre and the fact that this part of the stage would be higher than the downstage area, that closest to the audience.

USL

Upstage left (stage direction).

USR

Upstage right (stage direction).

Victorian

The period of theatre associated with the reign of Queen Victoria.

wings
The sides of the stage from which entrances and exits can be made.

Extension Activity

Glossary update

You may come across other words and phrases that you think should be included in a glossary to support this course. Make a list, and there will be opportunities to share your words and phrases through our website and blog.

Further reading, viewing and useful websites

FURTHER READING

This list is not exhaustive, and most of these books you can dip in and out of rather than read from cover to cover. Other books and publications feature at the end of each section. All of them are great for research and expanding your knowledge of the art of the theatre, not only for the AS year but onwards through the A2 course and into the future.

New thinking is being explored all the time in publications, and sometimes theatre styles go out of fashion very quickly. Look out too for newspaper articles and features on actors, directors or theatre companies – these appear more regularly than you think – for views and opinions on the changing state of theatre. The website that accompanies this book will also be exploring and reviewing new publications on a regular basis.

Benedetti, Jean (1982) *Stanislavski: An Introduction*, London: Methuen.
Bentley, Eric (1996) *The Life of the Drama*, London: Applause.
Berry, Cicely (2001) *Text in Action*, London: Virgin Books.
Billington, Michael (2007) *State of the Nation*, London: Faber & Faber.
Bond, Edward (2000) *Selections from the Notebooks*, London: Methuen.
Braun, Edward (1982) *The Director and the Stage*, London: Methuen.
Brook, Peter (1989) *The Shifting Point*, London: Methuen.
—— (1995) *There Are No Secrets*, London: Methuen.
—— (2008) *The Empty Space*, London: Penguin.
Callow, Simon (1984) *Being an Actor*, London: Methuen.
Esslin, Martin (1987) *The Theatre of the Absurd*, Harmondsworth: Penguin.
Fuegi, John (1995) *The Life and Times of Bertolt Brecht*, London: Flamingo.
Gottfried, Martin (2003) *Arthur Miller, A Life*, London: Faber and Faber.
Grotowski, Jerry (1975) *Towards a Poor Theatre*, London: Methuen.
Hall, Peter (2000) *Exposed by the Mask: Form and Language in Drama*, London: Oberon Books.
Hirst, David L. (1985) *Edward Bond*, Basingstoke: Macmillan.
Holdsworth, Nadine (2006) *Joan Littlewood*, London: Routledge.
Leach, Robert (2006) *Theatre Workshop: Joan Littlewood and the Making of Modern Theatre*, Exeter: University of Essex Press.
Merlin, Bella (2007) *The Complete Stanislavsky Toolkit*, London: Nick Hern Books.

Miller, Arthur (1987) *Timebends: A Life*, London: Methuen.

Sierz, Aleks (2001) *In-Yer-Face Theatre*, London: Faber & Faber.

Stafford-Clark, Max (1989) *Letters to George*, London: Nick Hern Books.

Stanislavsky, Konstantin (1937) *An Actor Prepares*, London: Methuen.

—— (2008) *An Actor's Work; My Life in Art*, London: Routledge.

Thoss, Michael (1994) *Brecht for Beginners*, trans. Jean Benedetti, New York: Writers and Readers.

Willett, John (1978) *Brecht on Theatre*, London: Methuen.

SUGGESTED VIEWING

There are a number of films with a theatrical slant to them which give an excellent feel of the period in which they are set.

Looking for Richard (dir. Al Pacino, 1996). Pacino researching his role as Richard III, featuring a host of well-known faces. As a 'diary of rehearsal', gives a real insight into the process.

Shakespeare in Love (dir. John Madden, 1998). A romp through Shakespearian England, giving a vivid picture of London at the time and a version of the theatre of the day.

Stage Beauty (dir. Richard Eyre, 2004). Moving on from *Shakespeare in Love,* the position of the greatest 'female' actor is in doubt when women are allowed to appear on the stage. A sense of the period and the politics of the time is evoked.

The Dresser (dir. Peter Yates, 1983). Based on a stage play, the story of an actor manager and his dresser as they cross the country to present the great works in provincial theatres. An evocation of the time and the changing theatrical styles.

Extension Activity

Reviewing performance

- If you watch more than one version of the same play – *Hamlet,* for example – you can do a compare-and-contrast activity on acting style, design elements and interpretation. What did you as a student of drama recognise from the different director's slants on the same source material?
- Write a review – up to 1,000 words – of a film you have watched from the list. Focus on the following elements:

- acting;
- design;
- interpretation.

There are also numerous versions of well-known plays available – either as filmed versions of the stage production or as film interpretations. Some are more useful than others, but all will provide some insight into the play itself and the time period in which it is set and filmed. Again, this list is not exhaustive, but there is a real range of experiences here, all of which are available on DVD at the time of writing.

A Day in the Death of Joe Egg (dir. Peter Medak, 1972; dir. Robin Lough, 2002 – TV). A film version of Peter Nicholl's play about a couple coping with life with a severely handicapped daughter.

A Midsummer Night's Dream (dir. William Dieterle and Max Reinhardt, 1935; dir. Peter Hall, 1968; dir. Michael Hoffman, 1999).

A Streetcar Named Desire (dir. Elia Kazan, 1951). Film version of Tennessee William's play that brought Marlon Brando to prominence; there is also a later made-for-television version.

A Taste of Honey (dir. Tony Richardson, 1961). Film version of Shelagh Delaney's first and most famous play. A real slice of 'kitchen sink drama' here with great performances and a period feel to it.

Agnes of God (dir. Norman Jewison, 1985). Film version of this controversial play set in a convent. Agnes, a novice, is pregnant and she says her child is the son of God. Powerful performances.

East (dir. Steven Berkoff, 2000). Film of the stage production of Berkoff's play. This is Berkoff at his most expressive – and there are some stunning physical theatre set pieces. Beware: very strong language.

Hamlet (dir. Laurence Olivier, 1948; dir. Tony Richardson, 1969; dir. Franco Zeffirelli, 1990; dir. Kenneth Branagh, 1996).

King Lear (dir. Peter Brook, 1971; dir. Michael Elliott, 1983). The 2007 stage version with Ian McKellen is available in 2008 or 2009.

Macbeth (dir. Orson Welles, 1948; dir. Roman Polanski, 1971).

Romeo and Juliet (dir. Franco Zeffirelli, 1968; dir. Baz Luhrmann, 1996).

Salome (dir. Steven Berkoff, 1992). Berkoff's take on Oscar Wilde's play. A film of a stage production that contains all the Berkoff hallmarks but here applied to somebody else's script.

The Caretaker (dir. Clive Donner, 1963). Film version of Pinter's most famous play. Controversial at the time and still able to shock with its undercurrent of violence.

The Crucible (dir. Nicholas Hytner, 1996). Film version of Arthur Miller's classic of witch-hunting in seventeenth-century Salem. Very faithful adaptation of the original.

The Entertainer (dir. Tony Richardson, 1960). Film version of John Osborne's play about the demise of a way of life for a variety performer. Great for the performance by Laurence Olivier in the role of Archie Rice.

The Glass Menagerie (dir. Irving Rapper, 1950; dir. Paul Newman, 1987). Film version of the Tennessee Williams play. Faithful to the original in content, if not always in style.

The Importance of Being Earnest (dir. Anthony Asquith, 1952). Film version of Oscar Wilde's play. A bit old and creaky now but it represents really well the language and comedy of the situation Wilde establishes. There is more than one version of the play on film, including a recent one with Rupert Everett (dir. Oliver Parker, 2002).

The Trial (dir. Steven Berkoff, 2002). Filmed stage version of Berkoff's adaptation of Kafka's novel. Has all the hallmarks of Berkoff's work.

Who's Afraid of Virginia Woolf (dir. Mike Nichols, 1966). Film version of Albee's acerbic dissection of a couple at war. Great performances from Richard Burton and Elizabeth Taylor.

USEFUL WEBSITES AT THE TIME OF WRITING

Look out for updates on our own website that supports and expands on our ideas in this book.

Big Brum, www.bigbrum.org.uk

Big Brum Theatre in Education (TIE) has been working in Birmingham and the West Midlands since 1982. The Company tours throughout the region to schools and colleges, working with pupils and students across the full age range. Big Brum tours two TIE programmes a year (one in the autumn term, and the other in the spring and summer terms) and offers other more specific projects to the education sector.

Bruvvers, www.bruvvers.co.uk

The north-east's foremost touring company. Bruvvers have been taking popular theatre to the community for more than thirty-five years. They are based in Newcastle upon Tyne, giving approximately 250 performances per year and playing to more than 40,000 people. They are an ensemble company with at least three plays in repertoire at any one time. Their shows are exciting and original and are aimed at all the family; they also help with workshops, festivals, conferences, teaching, enabling and passing on skills to all age ranges.

Donmar Warehouse, www.donmarwarehouse.com

The Donmar Warehouse is a 250-seat subsidised theatre located in the heart of London's West End, close to Covent Garden with a reputation as one of the UK's leading producing theatres. Actors are queuing up to work in its intimate, challenging space. As well as presenting at least six productions a year at its home in Covent Garden, the Donmar presents work nationally and internationally.

DV8, www.DV8.co.uk

DV8 Physical Theatre was formed in 1986 and is led by Lloyd Newson. To date, the company has produced fifteen highly acclaimed dance pieces, which have toured internationally, and five award-winning films for television. Exciting, challenging and, to some, controversial work that pushes back the boundaries in style, form and content.

Edexcel, www.edexcel.org.uk

The website of the Examination Board, constantly updated and a source of very useful information in relation to the range of qualifications on offer.

Frantic Assembly, www.franticassembly.co.uk

Frantic Assembly was formed in 1994. Since then it has toured extensively throughout the UK and abroad. The company has built its reputation as one of the country's most exciting and innovative companies. By producing thrilling, energetic and challenging theatre, the company creates a theatrical experience that reflects the way we live.

Guardian, www.guardian.co.uk

The home of the newspaper and great for online updates of what is going on in the world around you – including excellent coverage of the arts.

Hull Truck, www.hulltruck.co.uk

Established in 1971, Hull Truck is one of only six producing theatres in the Yorkshire region, and has been offering a range of performances and workshops from its base in Hull since 1983. Throughout its history, Hull Truck has continued to push artistic boundaries as a pioneering force of contemporary British theatre. Arguably, the company is most famous for John Godber and *Bouncers*.

Kaos Theatre, www.kaostheatre.com

The home of Kaos Theatre Company, under the artistic direction of Xavier Levet. Always worth a visit, and Kaos will thrill, surprise and shock, often in equal measure. This is what theatre is all about.

Kneehigh, www.kneehigh.co.uk

From its home in Cornwall, Kneehigh Theatre has built a reputation for creating vigorous and popular theatre for audiences throughout the UK and beyond. In Cornwall, Kneehigh created theatre for families in locations within their communities and from these simple beginnings, the company now finds itself celebrated as one of Britain's most exciting touring theatre companies. They create vigorous, popular theatre for a broad spectrum of audiences, using a multi-talented group of performers. A spontaneous sense of risk and adventure produces extraordinary dramatic results. Themes explored by Kneehigh are universal and local, epic and domestic, with recent acclaimed productions as diverse as *Brief Encounter*, *Tristan and Yseult* and *A Matter of Life and Death*.

National Theatre, www.nationaltheatre.org.uk

The National Theatre in London. A powerhouse of performance, incorporating an exciting mix of productions of classic and contemporary pieces. Well worth a visit in its own right with organised tours and talkback sessions offered on a regular basis. The good thing is it is not as expensive as you might think!

Northern Broadsides, www.northern-broadsides.co.uk

Formed in 1992 by Artistic Director Barrie Rutter, Northern Broadsides is a multi-award winning touring company based in Halifax, West Yorkshire. The company has built up an excellent reputation performing Shakespeare and classical texts with an innovative, popular and regional style. It could be said that Northern Broadsides' work is characterised by its vitality and humour, the passion of the performers, a refreshing ensemble style which adds tangible coherence to the performances and precise direction which results in work of great clarity and simplicity.

National Youth Theatre, www.nyt.org.uk

If you are aged between thirteen and twenty-one, the National Youth Theatre, Britain's premier youth theatre company, is just the place for you! Look out for audition information that is sent into schools and colleges on a regular basis and visit the website for up-to-date information of forthcoming projects. The National Youth Theatre performed at the handover ceremony following the 2008 Olympics.

Official London Theatre, www.officiallondontheatre.co.uk

A great way of keeping up with what is happening on the London stage with news, reviews, updates and offers. It is worth dipping into this site on a regular basis.

Royal Court Theatre, www.royalcourttheatre.com

The Royal Court is a world leader in theatre, producing new plays of the highest quality, encouraging new writers and challenging the nature of theatre of our time. Dedicated to new work by innovative writers from the UK and around the world, the theatre's pivotal role in promoting new voices is undisputed. From Bond to Churchill to Kane and Ravenhill, the Royal Court continues to excite and surprise its audiences.

Royal Shakespeare Company, www.rsc.org.uk

The website of the Royal Shakespeare Company is informative on a whole range of topics, including production news, interviews and regular updates on what is happening in the company.

Samuel French, www.samuelfrench-london.co.uk

If it is in print, it is probably available from Samuel French, world renowned for publishing acting editions of play scripts.

Shakespeare's Globe, www.shakespeares-globe.org

The site dedicated to the Globe Theatre and keeping you updated with production news, tour details and special offers. A very informative site, particularly when looking at Shakespeare's theatre and performance conditions.

Stagelight Training, www.stagelightingtraining.co.uk

An excellent source of information for the lighting candidate and wider training. You can also buy the comprehensive stage-lighting programme *Give Me Some Light* by Skip Mort on DVD.

Steven Berkoff, www.stevenberkoff.com

News, updates, reviews and special offers on publications and DVDs. Updated regularly, it presents Berkoff and something about his work and style very effectively.

Theatre Royal, www.theatreroyal.com

This is the website of the Theatre Royal in Plymouth, but there are a number of theatre royals around the country. Your local theatre will have a site similar to this one, keeping you updated on forthcoming productions.

The Stage, www.thestage.co.uk

The Stage is the trade paper that everybody involved in theatre either reads avidly – or avoids like the plague. It keeps you informed and updated but do not expect reviews to be too critical!

Index